THE GREAT
THAI
COOKBOOK

JACQUELINE BELLEFONTAINE

SIMON & SCHUSTER

LONDON · SYDNEY · NEW YORK · TOKYO · SINGAPORE · TORONTO

Photography by Peter Barry
Recipes by Jacqueline Bellefontaine
Watercolour illustrations by Sally Brewer
Designed by Alison Lee, Julie Smith and Helen Johnson
Edited by Jillian Stewart and Kate Cranshaw

CLB 4059
This edition published 1995 by Simon & Schuster
© 1995 CLB Publishing, Godalming, Surrey
All rights reserved
Colour separations by Advance Laser Graphic Arts, Hong Kong
Printed and bound in Singapore
ISBN 0-671-71391-4

Contents

Introduction

Thai food is a wonderful and exciting amalgamation of flavours and styles that results in a cuisine which, although influenced by several other countries, is quite unique to Thailand.

It is little wonder that Thai food is becoming more and more popular in Western countries. It isn't just the delicious flavours that are catching on. Thai cooking is perfect for our changing life style. Not only is it quick to prepare and cook, with many dishes taking only minutes to produce, it is also a healthy cuisine in which fresh vegetables play a predominant part. In addition, oil is generally only added in small quantities and fish and chicken are more important components than red meats.

Authentic tasting Thai food can easily be produced at home and with the many different styles of cooking – stir-frying, steaming, roasting and barbecuing – it need never become boring either. Similarities to both Chinese and Indian cuisine are easily recognised but generally speaking Thai food is hotter and spicier than Chinese and does not involve the long cooking of many Indian dishes.

Most of the ingredients used in Thai cooking are now easy to buy, especially if you have a good Oriental food store close at hand. The list of common ingredients on pages 12-15 will soon help you to familiarise yourself with many of the components.

The Regions

Geographically, Thailand can be divided into four very different major regions which accounts for the cuisine's strong regional variations.

The North
This rugged, mountainous region shares its border with Myanmar (Burma) and Laos, whose own cuisines have influenced some northern dishes. Glutinous rice is preferred to the fluffier fragrant rice more common elsewhere in Thailand. In contrast to the more usual method of eating rice, glutinous rice is shaped into balls with the fingers and dipped in other dishes before being eaten. Coconut milk is not so commonly used in dishes from the north, and although some dishes are highly seasoned, curries are generally milder than those in the central and northeast regions. A hot chilli dip is nevertheless always served for those who enjoy fiery flavours.

The North-East
Despite accounting for almost a third of the area and containing seven of the most populated provinces of Thailand, the soil in the north-east is poor and in many areas only sufficient to provide a subsistence living. The region suffers from prolonged droughts and when the rain does come it often results in heavy flooding. Temperatures too can be extreme and despite considerable agricultural progress being made, real hardship is still prevalent. Spicy meat dishes are a speciality, although they tend to be reserved for special occasions due to the scarcity of meat. Freshwater fish and shrimps are the main protein providers. Chillies are used in vast quantities, perhaps to help mask the inferior quality of some of the ingredients, and as a result the cuisine is very hot and spicy.

The Central Plains
In great contrast to the infertile soil of the northeast, the central plains form a flat, fertile basin, protected on three sides by mountains. The area is veined with rivers and canals to irrigate the land, and it is here that the world-renowned Thai fragrant rice, sometimes known as jasmine rice, is grown for home use and export. As well as rice, many varieties of fruit and vegetables are grown on the fertile soil. Dishes are usually accompanied with plain, steamed, fragrant rice or a rice dish of some kind. Basil, garlic and coriander are used in abundance and coconut milk also features strongly in recipes from this region. With Bangkok city in the region the area is truly multicultural and many of the dishes reflect the influences of other countries, while retaining their own unique Thai flavour.

The South
A long peninsula stretching like a long twisted finger down to Malaysia, the south is a rich mixture of orchards, vegetable and rice fields, and plantations of rubber trees and coconut palms. Not surprisingly, coconut milk is used in many of the dishes from the south and coconut oil is often used for frying. With two

coastlines totalling 1,625 miles there is a rich abundance of seafood. The majority of the Thai Muslim population live in the south and Indian cuisine is therefore a strong influence, seen in dishes such as the famous Mussaman curry. Raw vegetables are served with most meals and the cuisine is very hot, although perhaps not quite as hot as that of the northeast.

Cooking Techniques

There is nothing difficult about cooking Thai-style, nor is there any need to buy lots of specialist equipment – a few readily-available utensils are all that are needed. Stir-frying, steaming, boiling and frying are the main methods of cooking and these are familiar to most people in the West.

Equipment

A wok (Kata) is the most commonly used cooking utensil and although a large frying pan can be used, it

is worthwhile investing in this inexpensive piece of equipment if you enjoy Oriental-style cuisine.

The addition of a bamboo steamer, which is placed directly in the wok, is useful but you can improvise by placing a plate or colander over a saucepan of gently simmering water and covering with a lid to prevent the steam escaping.

Thais use a wire mesh basket on a bamboo handle for lifting foods out of the pan, but a slotted draining spoon is just as good.

You will also need a couple of saucepans and some sharp knives. Thais use a large cleaver for most of the preparation, even the intricate carvings for garnishes used on special occasions, but you will probably find it easier and safer to employ a good cook's knife.

A pestle and mortar is a necessity if you intend to prepare your own curry pastes. A food processor is generally unable to cope with the small quantities of spices used, though a mini-processor works well and cuts down on preparation time.

Stir-Frying

The secret of good stir-frying is to cook the food quickly over a high heat, keeping it constantly on the move to prevent it from burning. The high sides of a wok allow a large amount of food to be stirred whilst cooking without the food flying out of the pan. The ingredients should be added in quick succession, so it is essential to prepare all the ingredients for the recipe before beginning to cook. Indeed, you will find that the majority of the time taken to produce a Thai meal is in the preparation.

Preparing the Ingredients

Some of the ingredients used in Thai cooking need to be prepared before use. Here is how to prepare and use some of the less familiar ingredients:

Chillies

A word of caution. Handle chillies with care as their juice is a very strong irritant. It is a good idea to wear disposable or rubber gloves when cutting them [1].

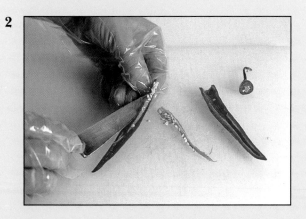

In all cases, wash hands very well after preparing, as even a tiny amount of the juice can cause considerable discomfort if it comes into contact with your eyes or mouth. If you prefer a milder flavour, discard the seeds [2] which contain much of the heat, and remember that, generally speaking, the smaller the chilli the stronger it will be. If you do not like your food too hot, you can still enjoy Thai cuisine, just add the chillies with caution.

Coconut Milk

If you are unable to buy coconut milk, make your own by combining 4oz/120g desiccated coconut with 420ml/¾ pint warm water, milk or half milk/half water. Whiz in a food processor for a few seconds. Allow to stand for 20 minutes then strain through a piece of muslin, squeezing out as much liquid as you can.

Fish Sauce

If unavailable, make your own substitute by pounding together canned anchovy fillets with a little sugar. Add a few spoonfuls of soy sauce and allow to stand for at least 30 minutes. Strain before using.

Fresh Root Ginger

Peel or scrape the skin away, then slice, chop or grate as required [3].

Lemon Grass

To use, cut away the grassy top and hard root [4]. Discard the tough outer leaves. Bruise the stem to release the flavour by pushing down hard on the blade of a knife, or thinly slice the central tender core [5].

Tamarind

The juice needs to be extracted from the tamarind pulp before use. To extract the juice, use about 1 part tamarind to 2 parts water. Soak the pulp in warm water for about 20-30 minutes, mashing occasionally against the side of the bowl. Strain through a sieve, pushing the juice out of the pulp with a spoon [6]. Scrape the underside of the sieve and add to the liquid. It is best used the same day.

Garnishes

Thais believe that food must please the eye as well as the taste buds and they will take great care in the presentation of dishes, all of which are usually garnished, even if only with a sprig of fresh coriander or a sprinkling of chopped coriander. Garnishing increases the enjoyment of a meal and in the following section you will find a guide to preparing a number of simple garnishes used throughout this book.

How to Make Simple Garnishes

Chilli 'Flowers'

These are made by cutting two or more times through the chilli from the tip, almost to the base. Place on a chopping board, hold at the stem and use a sharp knife to make the lengthways cuts [1]. Place in a bowl of iced water [2] and leave for about 1 hour or until required. The ends of the chilli will curl outwards to produce a flower-like effect [3]. These can be made with large or small chillies. Removing the seeds will also help the ends to curl.

3

4

5

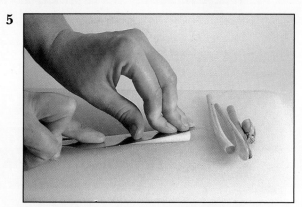

6

1

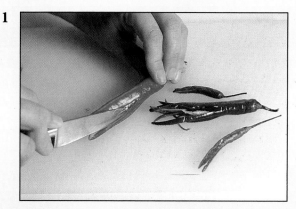

2

3

9

Spring Onion 'Brushes'

1

2

3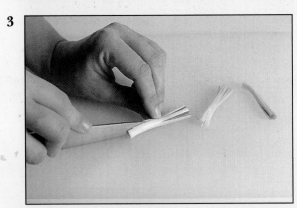

4

Chilli and Spring Onion Curls

1

Carrot Twigs

1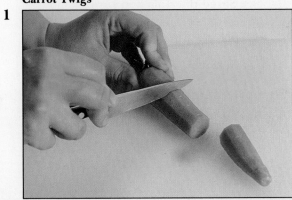

2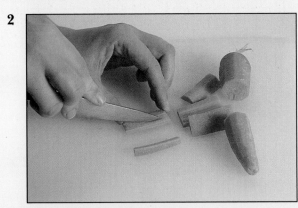

3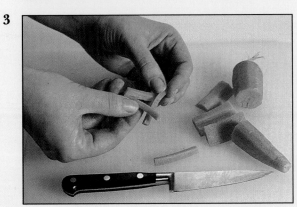

Spring Onion 'Brushes'

A similar effect to chilli 'flowers' can be achieved with spring onions. First, trim away the top of the onion, leaving a piece about 5-7cm/2-3 inches. Trim away the root [1]. Make cuts from the green end leaving the onion joined together at the root end [2]. Alternatively, make smaller cuts from both ends, not quite meeting in the middle [3]. Place in iced water to make the ends curl [4]. When required, remove and shake off excess water.

Chilli and Spring Onion Curls

These are attractive scattered over a dish. Cut the stem off the chilli, trim and discard the root and top part of spring onions. Shred the chilli and spring onion lengthways. Place in iced water until curled [1].

Carrot Twigs

Cut a 5cm/2-inch section from a carrot [1], then cut into thin slices lengthways to form rectangles. Take one slice of the carrot and make a cut from each end almost to the opposite end [2]. Twist the two outer strips so that they cross over [3]. Repeat with remaining carrot slices. You can also make twigs from a piece of lemon rind or slices of cucumber.

Banana Leaves

These are often cut into attractive shapes to line a plate, or used as a garnish. If available, wipe clean and cut into desired shape with scissors or pinking shears.

Planning and Serving a Thai Meal

In Thailand all the dishes are served at once, and a typical meal consists of soup, a curry, a steamed dish, a fried dish and a salad. These would be served with one or two sauces or dips and plain rice. Rice is a staple food in Thailand and plain rice is always served with a curry or soup, whereas a more sophisticated rice dish, such as Thai fried rice, would often be served as a light meal in itself.

Starters are a Western idea, but we have included suggestions for dishes which could be served first if wished. Desserts are usually only served at Thai banquets and on special occasions, but a number of sweet dishes are sold by street vendors at all times of the day.

Traditionally, a Thai meal is served at a low table with pillows and cushions to sit on. Each guest is given a plate, a fork and a spoon and if soup is to be served, a small bowl would also be provided with a ceramic, Chinese-style spoon. Each diner takes a serving of rice to which they would then add a small amount of one dish, and after eating this they would then move onto the next dish. Generally speaking, dishes are not mixed on the plate, but it is quite acceptable to eat the dishes in whatever order you please. Thais eat from the spoon and generally only use the fork to mix the dish with rice and to push the food onto a spoon. Of course how you serve the meal is entirely up to you, as the enjoyment of the food is the most important thing.

The easy, relaxed manner of eating Thai-style makes it the perfect cuisine for informal entertaining, and indeed, in Thailand, eating alone is considered one of life's great misfortunes. So armed with this book and a few essential ingredients, why not invite a few friends round to discover the joys of Thai cuisine.

The Ingredients

Don't be put off Thai cookery by the unusual ingredients used. When you look in the shops, you may be surprised just how many are now readily available. As Thai food becomes more popular, even the supermarkets are stocking such delights as coconut milk, red and green curry pastes, fresh root ginger and straw mushrooms. An Oriental food store is a good source of the more unusual ingredients. Some ingredients can be substituted or sometimes left out altogether, but the finished dish becomes less authentic.

The following list of main ingredients used in Thai cuisine will help make identifying them in the shops easier and also give guidance on suitable substitutes.

Basil – Several types of basil are used in Thailand, but they all taste different to our own, so use the real thing if you can find it or substitute home-grown basil for a different, but equally delicious, flavour. When adding to a dish, it is best to tear the leaves rather than cut them as this releases more flavour into the dish.

Baby Aubergines – A number of different varieties of small, round aubergines are used in Thailand. Unfortunately these are difficult to find in the West. You may be able to find these baby white or green aubergines in Oriental food stores. If unavailable, substitute our purple aubergine cut into chunks.

Banana Leaves – These large leaves are used for wrapping food in before steaming or baking. They impart a delicate flavour (and sometimes colour) to the food being cooked in them. Before using, wash the leaves well and soften, if necessary, by dipping in boiling water. The leaves are available fresh, usually folded up in large plastic bags, in the refrigerated sections of some Thai grocers. If unavailable, substitute baking parchment or foil as a wrapping. The leaves are also cut into decorative shapes and used as a garnish (see Garnishes).

Bok Choy – This variety of Chinese cabbage has stout white stems and bright green leaves, both of which are eaten. Its delicate flavour lends itself to a variety of cooking methods, including stir-frying, braising and steaming. It is sometimes available in large supermarkets as well as Oriental food stores, but if unavailable substitute ordinary Chinese cabbage.

Chillies – Chillies provide the heat in Thai dishes. The type most commonly used in Thai cooking are called 'Birds Eye' chillies and at only 1.25cm/½-inch long they are very hot. Green chillies are hotter than red chillies of the same size and, generally speaking, the smaller the chilli the hotter it is. Jars of ready-chopped chillies are very convenient for Thai cooking although whole dried and crushed chillies may also be used. Handle chillies with great care as their juice is a very strong irritant (see Cooking Techniques).

Coriander – Fresh coriander or Chinese parsley is used in many Asian cuisines. In Thailand, the root and stem are also used in cooking, particularly to flavour curries. Unfortunately, coriander is usually trimmed of its roots in this country, but do at least use the chopped stems. The leaves are often used to garnish a dish either whole or chopped and scattered over the top. Coriander seeds are also used dried as a spice.

Coconut and Coconut Milk – The flavour of coconut is a distinctive characteristic of Thai food. Coconut milk is most commonly used, and this should not be confused with the water from the inside of the coconut. Coconut milk is made from the shredded meat of the coconut. Canned coconut milk can now be bought in many supermarkets. Thick and thin coconut milk and coconut cream are all used in Thai recipes. When using canned coconut milk it is quite easy to obtain all these different 'grades' from the same can. Coconut milk separates in the can into layers; the top layer, the cream, is very thick and can be scooped off leaving the thin milk underneath. To obtain thick milk the contents of the can just need to be stirred together. Opened cans will only keep 1 or 2 days in the refrigerator, but coconut milk does freeze well so this is the best way to store it. Coconut powder is also fairly easy to find in supermarkets: make this up as directed on the packet. Alternatively, blocks of creamed coconut can be dissolved in water to make the milk. If you still have difficulty finding it in the shops you can make your own (See Cooking Techniques).

Curry Paste – Glancing through the recipes, it is obvious that red and green curry pastes are used frequently. Green curry paste is the hotter of the two as it uses the small, very hot serrano chillies. Both pastes are made in the same way by pounding chillies and spices together in a pestle and mortar to form a paste. Ready-made curry pastes are very convenient and can now be found in many large supermarkets as well as Oriental stores. However, home-made curry pastes do have a superior flavour so recipes are included in the Pastes and Dipping Sauces section. A mini-food processor is useful for avoiding the elbow work. For dishes with an Indian influence yellow curry paste is used – its colour comes from the turmeric used in the mix. Curry pastes keep well and it always a good idea to prepare double the quantity and refrigerate it in airtight glass jars for future use.

Dried Shrimps – These tiny shrimps are boiled and then sun-dried. They are best stored in airtight glass jars as they have a very pungent smell. Used extensively in Thai cooking, they are widely available in Oriental food stores.

Fish Sauce – Fish sauce is added to most dishes and eliminates the need for salt (soy sauce is used in a similar way in Chinese cooking). It is now available in many supermarkets, but if you are unable to find it make your own (see Cooking Techniques).

Five-Spice Powder – Often known as Chinese five-spice powder, this blend of powdered spices made from star anise, cassia bark, Sichuan peppercorns, cloves and fennel seeds is available from some large supermarkets as well as Oriental food stores.

Galangal (greater galangal) – A cousin of ginger, galangal is similar in appearance but has a milder, more perfumed flavour. Used in the same way as

ginger, it is available fresh or dried from Oriental food stores. Dried, it is sold as a powder known as Laos, (the fresh root is sometimes known by this name as well). If unavailable, substitute ginger, which will give a slightly different flavour, or omit from the recipe.

Garlic – Used extensively as an ingredient in Thai cooking, fresh garlic is also chopped and fried until golden and used as a garnish. Although the garlic found in Thailand is different from our own (it is smaller and sweeter), ordinary garlic works just as well.

Garlic Chives – These are flat green chives with a very strong flavour and smell. Substitute ordinary chives or the tops of spring onions and add a little extra garlic to the dish. Garlic chives are traditionally used in the classic noodle dish Pad Thai.

Ginger – Ginger is available fresh, dried, ground and candied. Fresh root ginger is used in many Thai dishes (see Cooking Techniques) and is now readily available. A slice is sometimes added to a recipe to give a subtle flavour, but it should be removed before serving.

Green Papaya (Pawpaw) – Like mango, papaya is eaten ripe as a dessert, or used unripe as a savoury ingredient. Look out for the larger unripe green papaya in Oriental food stores to make the deliciously refreshing Green Papaya Salad.

Jasmine Water – This is used in Thai cooking in the same way as rosewater or orange flower water in Indian cuisine. It is made from the flowers of a highly scented type of jasmine and adds a perfumed fragrance to the recipes.

Kaffir Lime Leaves – These shiny, dark green leaves with a distinctive figure-of-eight shape are an important flavouring in authentic Thai cooking. Used in a similar way to bay leaves they can be added whole or torn in half to infuse flavour to the dish, or shredded for a garnish. They are available fresh, frozen or dried from some Oriental food stores. Dried lime leaves add very little flavour to the dish and are best avoided. Shredded lime zest can be substituted, but the flavour will not be quite as authentic.

Lemon Grass – Lemon grass imparts a delicious lemony tang to dishes and although lemon zest or juice can be substituted, the resulting flavour is not quite the same. It has a fibrous texture so is either bruised and used to infuse a dish with its flavour (in the way a bay leaf is used) or sliced very finely (see Cooking Techniques). It is also used pounded in curry pastes. Lemon grass is available dried but this has little flavour or aroma so should be avoided. However, fresh lemon grass freezes well and is sometimes available in larger supermarkets as well as most Oriental food stores. To freeze fresh lemon grass simply trim away the outer leaves and freeze for future use.

Limes – Fresh lime juice is a basic ingredient and the fruit is often used for a garnish. Lemon can be substituted if limes are unavailable.

Long Beans – As the name suggests, long beans grow to a length of about 60cm/2 feet. They are similar in flavour to French or fine beans, which can be used as a substitute if long beans are unavailable.

Noodles – A noodle dish is usually served at every Thai meal. There are many types eaten in Thailand but the most important are rice, cellophane and egg noodles. Rice noodles are made from rice and are available dried in different sizes. Cellophane or glass noodles are made from mung beans and are almost transparent in appearance. Egg noodles are made from egg and wheat flour and are available both fresh and dried, and again come in various widths. They are used in soups and stir-fried dishes.

Palm Sugar – A thick brown sugar made from the boiled sap of the palmyra palm tree or the coconut palm. It is almost wet in texture and is available in tubs or cans from Oriental stores. Substitute an unrefined sugar such as light or dark muscovado sugar if unavailable.

Prawns – For cooking it is best to use uncooked prawns. These are available frozen from Oriental stores and some supermarkets. If you are unable to buy them, use cooked prawns, add at the last moment, and cook over a low heat just long enough to heat them through. Never over-cook prawns as they become tough.

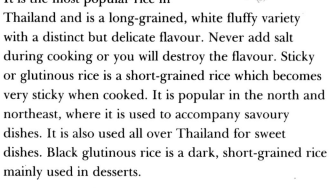

Rice – The backbone of Thai food, no meal is complete without a rice dish. There are three main types of rice used. Jasmine, also known as Thai fragrant rice, is world renowned. It is the most popular rice in Thailand and is a long-grained, white fluffy variety with a distinct but delicate flavour. Never add salt during cooking or you will destroy the flavour. Sticky or glutinous rice is a short-grained rice which becomes very sticky when cooked. It is popular in the north and northeast, where it is used to accompany savoury dishes. It is also used all over Thailand for sweet dishes. Black glutinous rice is a dark, short-grained rice mainly used in desserts.

Salted Black Beans – These are fermented, salted soya beans. Sold in small plastic bags in Oriental food stores, they will keep well if transferred to an airtight jar. Wash and dry the beans prior to using and crush or chop them before adding to a dish. If unavailable, a little black bean sauce can be used as a substitute.

Shallots – The Thai shallot has a purple/pink tinge and a strong flavour. Any variety of shallots can be used as an alternative, or use a little chopped onion.

Shrimp Paste – Available in small jars from Oriental food stores, this paste is used to add flavour and saltiness to many Thai dishes. It has a very pungent smell so should be kept in an airtight glass jar. Before using, it should be fried – this is usually included in the recipe instructions.

Soy Sauce – Used as a seasoning in some Thai dishes. Use light or dark soy according to your own preference. Light soy sauce is sweeter and saltier than the dark soy sauce.

Spring Onions – Often used as a garnish (see Garnishes) and sometimes to impart their mild onion flavour to a dish.

Spring Roll Wrappers – Available frozen from Oriental food stores, spring roll wrappers can be refrozen after cooking. Keep well wrapped when storing or using as they quickly dry out. If unavailable, filo pastry can be used for fried dishes and will give a similar result.

Star Anise – These star-shaped seed pods have a strong liquorice flavour. This spice is available whole or ground in some large supermarkets as well as Oriental food stores. If unobtainable, use fennel seeds as a substitute.

Straw Mushrooms – Available in cans from Oriental food stores and supermarkets. Substitute any other mushroom if straw mushrooms are unavailable.

Tamarind – Made from the ripe bean-like fruit of the tamarind tree, it gives a fruity-sour flavour to meat and fish dishes. Tamarind pulp is available in blocks from Oriental food stores and the juice is extracted for use in recipes (see Cooking Techniques). If unavailable, substitute lemon juice.

Turmeric – Used to add colour to many dishes, especially those of Indian or Muslim origin.

Wonton Wrappers – Also known as wonton skins, these are made from the same wheat flour and egg dough that is used to make egg noodles. The dough is rolled out until wafer thin and cut into squares. They are available fresh or frozen from Oriental food stores and like, spring roll wrappers, should be kept covered when using to prevent them drying out.

Chapter 1

Soups
&
Starters

Curry Parcels • Glass Noodle Soup • Thai Omelette
Rice Soup with Pork • Thai Spring Rolls • Beef Saté
Coconut Prawn Soup • Son-In-Law Eggs
Pork Wrapped in Noodles • Beef Noodle Soup
Mussels in Chilli Sauce • Thai Pork Stuffed Omelettes
Spicy Prawn Wraps • Chicken Coconut Soup

CURRY PARCELS

A tasty snack which can also
be served as a starter.

MAKES 18

225g/8oz chicken breasts
2 tbsps oil
1 small onion, finely chopped
225g/8oz cooked potato, diced
1 tbsp Red or Green Curry Paste (see Pastes
 and Dipping Sauces)
2 tsps sugar
18 wonton wrappers
Oil for deep-frying
Cucumber slices, to garnish

1. Skin the chicken and chop finely. Heat the oil in a wok and stir-fry the onion and chicken for 3 minutes.

2. Stir in the potato, curry paste and sugar and fry for a few minutes. Remove the chicken mixture to a plate.

3. Place the wonton wrappers in front of you on a damp tea-towel to prevent them drying out too quickly. Spoon a little of the filling into the centre of one of the wrappers.

4. Dampen the edges with water. Pull up the edges of the pastry and pinch together, enclosing the filling. Repeat until you have used up all the filling.

5. Heat the oil for deep-frying in a clean wok and deep-fry a few parcels at a time for 3-4 minutes or until crisp and golden.

6. Drain on kitchen paper, and garnish with cucumber slices.

Step 4 Dampen the edges with water, pull up the edges of the pastry and pinch together to enclose the filling.

Step 3 Place the wonton wrappers on a tea-towel and spoon a little of the filling onto the centre of each wrapper.

Step 5 Deep-fry a few parcels at a time, for 3-4 minutes or until crisp and golden.

Cook's Notes

Time
Preparation takes 20 minutes and cooking takes 30 minutes.

Serving Idea
Serve with Sweet and Sour Dipping Sauce.

GLASS NOODLE SOUP

This attractive soup contains spicy meatballs and, of course,
the cellophane noodles which give the dish its name.

SERVES 4

2 tbsps oil
2 cloves garlic, thinly sliced
60g/2oz dried cellophane noodles
225g/8oz skinned and boned chicken breast
2 tbsps Green Curry Paste (see Pastes and Dipping
  Sauces)
2 tbsps fish sauce
3 tbsps cornflour
1 tbsp chopped coriander leaves
1litre/1¾ pints chicken stock
225g/8oz bok choy, shredded
4 spring onions, cut into 2.5cm/1-inch pieces

1. Heat the oil in a small frying pan or wok and fry the
garlic until golden. Remove with a slotted spoon and
drain on kitchen paper.

2. Place the noodles in a large bowl and cover with hot
water, allow to soak until softened, then drain.

3. Cut the chicken into chunks, place in a food
processor with the curry paste, fish sauce, cornflour
and coriander and process until very finely minced.

4. Remove the mixture from the processor and shape
into small balls.

5. Heat the stock in a large saucepan until boiling and
add the meatballs. Cook for 10-15 minutes, or until they
rise to the surface.

6. Add the softened noodles, bok choy and spring
onions and continue to cook for 5 minutes. Serve
sprinkled with the fried garlic slices.

Step 3 Place the chicken, curry paste, fish sauce, cornflour and coriander into a food processor and process until very finely minced.

Step 4 Shape the mixture into small balls.

Step 5 Cook the meatballs for 10-15 minutes, or until they rise to the surface.

Cook's Notes

Time
Preparation takes 15 minutes
and cooking takes 15-20 minutes.

Variation
Use other types of noodles.

THAI OMELETTE

In Thailand, omelettes are always served with a hot dipping sauce.

SERVES 4

6 eggs
2 tbsps fish sauce
1 tsp water
1 small red chilli, sliced
3 spring onions, sliced
2 tbsps oil
Banana leaves and chilli curls, to garnish

1. Place the eggs in a mixing bowl with the fish sauce and water and whisk until well combined and slightly frothy. Stir in the chilli and spring onions.

2. Heat the oil in a heavy-based frying pan and when a haze rises from the pan, pour in the egg mixture.

3. Reduce the heat and cook the egg mixture by pulling the egg from the side of the pan as it sets and letting

Step 1 Place the eggs in a mixing bowl with the fish sauce and water, and whisk until well combined and slightly frothy.

Step 1 Stir in the chillies and spring onions.

Step 3 Cook the egg mixture by pulling the egg from the side of the pan as it sets, and letting the uncooked mixture run underneath.

the uncooked mixture run to the edges of the pan.

4. When the egg mixture is almost set, place the pan under a preheated grill to brown the top.

5. Slide onto a serving plate and cut into wedges. Garnish with shapes cut from a banana leaf and chilli curls. Serve with a dipping sauce.

Cook's Notes

 Time
Preparation takes 10 minutes and cooking takes about 10 minutes.

Serving Idea
Serve as a quick lunch dish for 2.

RICE SOUP WITH PORK
(KHAO TOM MOO)

This dish often forms part of Thai breakfasts. Sometimes an egg is lightly poached in the soup just before serving.

SERVES 4

2 tbsps oil
2 cloves garlic, chopped
850ml/1½ pints pork or chicken stock
225g/8oz minced pork
340g/12oz cooked rice
2 sticks celery, sliced
2 spring onions, sliced
1 tbsp chopped coriander leaves and stem
1 tbsp fish sauce
Pinch of white pepper

Step 2 Add the pork, rice, celery and spring onions to the boiling stock and simmer gently for 15 minutes.

Step 3 Stir in the coriander, fish sauce and pepper.

Step 1 Heat the oil in a small frying pan or wok and fry the garlic until pale golden.

1. Heat the oil in a small frying pan or wok and fry the garlic until pale golden. Remove with a slotted spoon and drain on kitchen paper.

2. Put the stock in a large saucepan and bring to the boil. Add the pork, rice, celery and spring onions to the pan and simmer gently for 15 minutes.

3. Stir in the coriander, fish sauce and pepper. Serve sprinkled with the fried garlic.

Cook's Notes

Time
Preparation takes 10 minutes and cooking takes about 20 minutes.

Variation
Use chicken instead of pork and chop finely by hand or in a food processor.

Cook's Tip
Cooked rice freezes very well, and can be quickly reheated in boiling water or by microwaving or steaming.

THAI SPRING ROLLS (PO PIA TAUD)

Spring rolls have become so popular that they are now available at supermarket delicatessens. However, they are simple to make at home and will taste much better than the supermarket version.

MAKES ABOUT 12

2 tbsps oil
1 clove garlic, crushed
120g/4oz chopped pork
2 carrots, cut into thin sticks
2 sticks celery, cut into thin sticks
1 red or green chilli, chopped
4 spring onions, sliced
1 tsp grated fresh root ginger
1 tbsp chopped fresh coriander
1 tsp fish sauce
60g/2oz noodles, cooked
About 12 spring roll wrappers
Oil for deep-frying
Fresh coriander leaves, to garnish

1. Heat the oil in a wok or frying pan and fry the garlic, pork, carrots, celery and chilli for a few minutes until the pork is cooked and the vegetables are beginning to soften.

2. Stir in the spring onions, ginger, coriander, fish sauce and noodles; cook gently to heat through.

3. Place a spring roll wrapper on a work surface and position a small amount of the filling across one corner. Roll up, folding in the corners to completely enclose the filling. Fill one spring roll at a time and keep the remaining wrappers covered with a damp tea-towel to prevent them from drying out.

4. Just before serving, deep-fry the spring rolls in batches for 3-4 minutes or until crisp and golden. Garnish with fresh coriander and serve immediately.

Step 3 Place some filling across one corner of a spring roll wrapper and fold in the corners to completely enclose the filling.

Step 2 Stir the spring onions, ginger, coriander, fish sauce and noodles into the wok and heat through.

Step 4 Deep-fry the spring rolls for 3-4 minutes or until crisp and golden.

Cook's Notes

Time
Preparation takes 20 minutes and cooking takes 20 minutes.

Serving Idea
Serve with Sweet Chilli Sauce (see Pastes and Dipping Sauces).

Variation
Add chopped prawns or bean sprouts to the filling.

BEEF SATÉ (NUEA SATAY)

A very popular Thai dish which can also
be served as a light snack or as party food.

SERVES 4

225g/8oz sirloin steak
Grated rind and juice of 1 lime
1 tsp chopped fresh chilli
1 tbsp chopped fresh coriander
½ tsp ground turmeric
½ tsp ground cumin
2 tsps fish sauce
Oil for brushing
Chilli 'flowers' and spring onion 'brushes', to garnish

Saté Sauce
90g/3oz unsalted roasted peanuts
1 small red chilli
Juice of 1 lime
¼ tsp ground cumin
¼ tsp ground coriander
2 tbsps thick coconut milk
2 tbsps oil
1 small onion, finely chopped
Dash of fish sauce
30-60ml/2-4 tbsps water

Step 1 Thread the beef strips onto bamboo skewers.

Step 2 Pour the marinade over the beef and leave for at least 1 hour.

1. Cut the steak into thin slices and thread onto bamboo skewers. Place in a shallow dish.

2. Mix together the lime rind and juice, chilli, coriander, turmeric, cumin and fish sauce and pour over the beef. Turn to coat in the marinade and leave for at least 1 hour.

3. To prepare the sauce, place the peanuts, chilli, lime juice, spices and coconut milk in a pestle and mortar or food processor and grind to a paste.

4. Heat the oil in a saucepan and fry the onion until soft. Stir in the peanut mixture and add some fish sauce to taste. Add the marinade from the beef and a little water to form a thick sauce. Cook for 5 minutes, stirring constantly.

5. Brush the satés with oil and cook under a preheated grill for 3-5 minutes or until the beef is cooked through. Serve with the saté sauce. Garnish with the chilli and spring onions.

Cook's Notes

Time
Preparation takes 15 minutes, plus 1 hour marinating. Cooking takes 10 minutes.

Variation
Crunchy peanut butter can be used instead of ground peanuts.

Preparation
To make the cutting of the steak easier, partially freeze the meat. Cut across the grain to keep the meat tender.

COCONUT PRAWN SOUP

Soup is usually served as part of a full Thai meal,
but is also served at any time as a snack.

SERVES 4

1 stem of lemon grass
225g/8oz raw king prawns
1.1litres/2 pints fish stock
4 slices galangal
4 kaffir lime leaves, shredded
2 red or green chillies, chopped
1 tbsp fish sauce
225g/8oz skinned white fish fillets, cut into strips
140ml/¼ pint thick coconut milk

1. Thinly slice a piece of the lemon grass about 5cm/
2 inches long.

2. Peel the king prawns leaving just the tails.

3. Pull away the dark vein from the tails and discard.

4. Heat the stock in a large saucepan until almost
boiling and stir in the galangal, lime leaves, lemon
grass, chillies and fish sauce. Simmer for 2 minutes.

5. Add the fish strips and prawns and cook gently for 5
minutes.

Step 2 Peel the king
prawns leaving just
the tails.

Step 3 Pull away the
dark vein from the
prawn tails.

6. Stir in the coconut milk and continue cooking until
very hot, but do not allow to boil.

Cook's Notes

Time
Preparation takes 20 minutes
and cooking takes 10 minutes.

Cook's Tip
Use a firm-fleshed fish that won't
break up too much during cooking.

Variation
Ginger can be used instead of
galangal.

SON-IN-LAW EGGS
(KAI LEUK KOEY)

This popular and well-known Thai dish is traditionally made
with duck eggs, but hen eggs can be used instead.

SERVES 4

Sauce
140ml/¼ pint tamarind juice
75g/2½oz dark muscovado sugar
90ml/6 tbsps fish sauce

Oil for deep-frying
4 shallots, thinly sliced
4 cloves garlic, thinly sliced
4 hard-boiled eggs, peeled
Spring onion 'brushes' and chilli 'flowers', to garnish

1. Combine the sauce ingredients in a small saucepan
and heat gently, stirring until the sugar dissolves. Bring
to the boil, then reduce the heat and simmer gently for
5-10 minutes.

2. Heat the oil in a wok to 180°C/350°F. Add the
shallots and fry for 1-2 minutes until golden brown and
crisp. Remove with a slotted spoon and drain on
kitchen paper.

3. Add the garlic and fry for 1 minute until pale golden,
taking care not to allow it to burn. Drain on
kitchen paper.

4. Add the eggs to the wok and deep-fry for 5-10
minutes until golden and bubbly on all sides. Keep
turning the eggs so that they do not burn on the
bottom. When golden, remove from the oil and drain

Step 4 Add the eggs
to the hot oil and
deep-fry for 5-10
minutes. Keep
turning the eggs so
that they do not burn.

Step 5 Cut the eggs
in half lengthways
and arrange on a
serving plate.
Sprinkle the fried
shallots and garlic
over the top.

the eggs on kitchen paper.

5. Cut the eggs in half lengthways and arrange on a
serving plate. Sprinkle the fried shallots and garlic over
the egg. Serve the sauce in a separate bowl, or poured
over the eggs. Garnish with spring onion 'brushes' and
chilli 'flowers'.

Cook's Notes

Time
Preparation takes 20 minutes
and cooking takes 15-20 minutes.

Watchpoint
Allow the oil to cool before
removing it from the wok.

PORK WRAPPED IN NOODLES

Relatively mild in flavour, these crisp bundles
are served with a hot dipping sauce.

SERVES 4

225g/8oz minced pork
1 tsp ground coriander
1 tbsp fish sauce
1 small egg, beaten
90g/3oz rice noodles (vermicelli)
Oil for deep-frying
Whole chillies, to garnish

1. Mix together the pork, coriander and fish sauce until well combined, then add enough egg to bind. Roll the mixture into small balls and chill for 30 minutes.

2. Cover the noodles with warm water and soak for about 10 minutes to soften. Drain the noodles then

Step 2 Cover the noodles with warm water and leave to soak for about 10 minutes to soften.

Step 2 Drain the noodles then wrap several strands around each pork ball.

Step 1 Roll the pork mixture into small balls and chill for 30 minutes.

wrap several strands around each pork ball.

3. Heat the oil in a wok and deep-fry a few at a time for 3-4 minutes or until crisp and golden. Drain on kitchen paper and garnish with whole chillies.

Cook's Notes

Time
Preparation takes 20 minutes, plus 30 minutes chilling time. Cooking takes about 20 minutes.

Serving Idea
Serve with a hot dipping sauce such as Nam Prik or Sweet Chilli Sauce.

BEEF NOODLE SOUP

You can use any type of noodle in this recipe,
or substitute rice for a change.

SERVES 4

2 tbsps oil
225g/8oz sirloin steak, cut into thin strips
1 small onion, chopped
2 sticks celery, sliced diagonally
1.4 litres/2½ pints chicken or beef stock
1 tbsp chopped coriander root and stem
2 kaffir lime leaves
2.5cm/1-inch piece fresh root ginger, peeled and
    thinly sliced
1 tsp palm sugar
1 tbsp fish sauce
90g/3oz egg noodles
120g/4oz canned straw mushrooms (drained weight)
Chilli 'flowers', to garnish

1. Heat the oil in a wok or saucepan and fry the meat,

Step 2 Add the stock, coriander, lime leaves, ginger, sugar and fish sauce to the wok and bring to the boil.

onion and celery until the meat is cooked through and the vegetables are soft.

2. Add the stock, coriander, lime leaves, ginger, sugar and fish sauce. Bring to the boil.

3. Add the noodles and straw mushrooms and cook for 10 minutes. Serve piping hot, garnished with chilli 'flowers'.

Step 1 Fry the meat, onion and celery in a wok until the meat is cooked through and the vegetables are soft.

Step 3 Add the noodles and mushrooms and cook for 10 minutes.

Cook's Notes

Time
Preparation takes 15 minutes and cooking takes 20 minutes.

Cook's Tip
Partially freeze the beef to make slicing easier. Cut the meat across the grain to keep it tender.

MUSSELS IN CHILLI SAUCE

Seafood is an important part of the diet in Thailand.
In this recipe mussels are served in a simple chilli sauce.

SERVES 4

900g/2lbs live mussels
280ml/½ pint water
1 stem lemon grass, chopped
2.5cm/1-inch piece fresh root ginger, peeled and sliced
4 dried kaffir lime leaves

Chilli Sauce
3 large red chillies, chopped
1 tbsp chopped coriander root and stem
2 cloves garlic, crushed
2 tbsps oil
2 tbsps fish sauce
1 tbsp sugar
1 tbsp sweet basil, chopped
2 tsps cornflour mixed with a little water

Basil leaves and chilli flowers, to garnish

1. Scrub the mussels and remove the beards, discarding any mussels with broken shells or those that do not close when tapped.

2. Bring the water to the boil and add the lemon grass, ginger and lime leaves. Add the mussels, cover and

Step 2 Bring the water to the boil and add the lemon grass, ginger and lime leaves.

boil for 5-6 minutes or until the mussels open.

3. Drain, reserving 140ml/¼ pint of the cooking liquid. Discard any mussels that have not opened.

4. While the mussels are cooking start to prepare the sauce. Pound the chillies, coriander and garlic together in a pestle and mortar.

5. Heat the oil in a wok and fry the chilli mixture for a few minutes, then stir in the fish sauce, sugar and basil.

6. Add the reserved cooking liquid from the mussels and the cornflour mixture. Cook until slightly thickened.

7. Serve the mussels with the sauce poured over them. Garnish with basil leaves and chilli 'flowers'.

Step 1 Scrub the mussels and remove the beards.

Step 5 Fry the chilli mixture for a few minutes.

Cook's Notes

Time
Preparation takes 10 minutes and cooking takes 10-12 minutes.

Watchpoint
Do not overcook the mussels as they will become tough. Remove from the heat as soon as they open.

THAI PORK STUFFED OMELETTES
(KAI YAHT SAI)

Plain omelettes filled with a spicy pork mixture make a delicious
starter or snack. Serve with a dipping sauce.

SERVES 2

Filling
2 tbsps oil
1 small green chilli, sliced
1 clove garlic, crushed
2 shallots, chopped
120g/4oz minced pork
30g/1oz peeled prawns, chopped
2 tbsps fish sauce
1 large plum tomato, chopped
2 tsps sugar
Pinch of white pepper
2 tbsps chopped coriander leaves, stem and root

Omelettes
4 eggs
1 tbsp fish sauce
1 tsp water
2 tbsps oil

Chilli 'flowers', to garnish

1. To make the filling, heat the oil and fry the chilli, garlic and shallots for 3 minutes or until softened.

2. Add the minced pork and cook until it has changed colour, breaking it up as it cooks.

3. Add the remaining filling ingredients and stir-fry for 3-4 minutes. Keep warm whilst cooking the omelettes.

4. To make the omelettes, place the eggs in a mixing bowl with the fish sauce and water and whisk until well combined and slightly frothy.

5. Heat half the oil in a small heavy-based frying pan and when just hazing, pour in half the egg mixture. Reduce the heat and cook the egg mixture, pulling the egg from the side of the pan as it sets, and letting the uncooked mixture run to the edges of the pan.

6. When the egg mixture is almost set, gently flip it over to cook the top or place under a preheated grill to brown. Spoon half the pork mixture into the centre of the omelette and fold up to completely enclose. Transfer to a serving dish and keep warm. Make and fill a second omelette with the remaining egg and pork mixture. Serve with a dipping sauce and garnish with chilli 'flowers'.

Step 6 Spoon half the pork mixture into the centre of the omelette.

Step 6 Fold the omelette up to completely enclose the filling.

Cook's Notes

Time
Preparation takes 15 minutes and cooking takes 20-25 minutes.

Cook's Tip
If you have two small frying pans cook both omelettes at once.

SPICY PRAWN WRAPS

Use large, uncooked deep-water prawns for this dish – look out for them in the freezer cabinet in Oriental shops and large supermarkets.

SERVES 4

12 raw king prawns
1 clove garlic, crushed
1 stem lemon grass, finely sliced
1 red chilli, seeded and chopped
1 tsp grated fresh root ginger
Juice of 1 lime
12 small spring roll wrappers
Oil for deep-frying

Step 2 Cut through the back of the prawns without cutting right through the bodies.

1. Peel the prawns, removing their heads and body shells, but leaving the tail fins attached.

2. Remove the dark vein and 'butterfly' the prawns by cutting through the back of the prawns without cutting right through the bodies. Carefully open the prawns out.

3. Combine the garlic, lemon grass, chilli, ginger and lime juice in a shallow dish and add the prawns.

4. Turn the prawns so that they are coated in the

Step 4 Turn the prawns in the marinade to coat them. Refrigerate for 2 hours, turning occasionally.

marinade, then allow to marinate in the refrigerator for 2 hours, turning occasionally.

5. Just before serving, remove the prawns from the marinade and wrap each prawn in a spring roll wrapper, leaving the tail end sticking out.

6. Heat the oil to 180°C/350°F in a wok and fry the prawn wraps in batches for 3-4 minutes or until golden. Drain on kitchen paper.

Step 5 Remove the prawns from the marinade and wrap each in a spring roll wrapper, leaving the tail ends sticking out.

Cook's Notes

Time
Preparation takes 20 minutes, plus 2 hours marinating. Cooking takes about 12 minutes.

Serving Idea
Serve with a hot dipping sauce such as Nuoc Cham.

CHICKEN COCONUT SOUP
(TOM KHA GAI)

This is a rich aromatic soup, and its mild flavour makes it
particularly popular with those new to Thai food.

SERVES 4

1 chicken breast, skinned and boned
420ml/¾ pint thick coconut milk
280ml/½ pint chicken stock
6 slices galangal
2 red chillies, seeded and cut into strips
6 black peppercorns, crushed
4 kaffir lime leaves, torn in half
1 stem lemon grass, bruised
60ml/4 tbsps fish sauce
60ml/4 tbsps lime juice

Step 1 Cut the chicken into thin strips across the grain using a sharp knife.

1. Cut the chicken into thin strips across the grain, using a sharp knife.

2. Combine the coconut milk and chicken stock in a large saucepan and bring to the boil.

Step 2 Combine the coconut milk and chicken stock in a large saucepan and bring to the boil.

3. Reduce the heat to a simmer and add the chicken, galangal, chillies, peppercorns, lime leaves and lemon grass. Simmer gently for 15-20 minutes, or until the chicken is tender and cooked through.

4. Add the fish sauce and lime juice and serve.

Step 4 Add the fish sauce and lime juice then serve immediately.

Cook's Notes

Time
Preparation takes 10-15 minutes and cooking takes about 20 minutes.

Cook's Tip
To make the chicken easier to slice, partially freeze it so that it holds its shape to allow thin and even strips to be cut.

Chapter 2
Fish
&
Seafood

Fried Spice Fish • Stir-Fried Seafood
Thai Sweet Sour Fish • Steamed Fish • Grilled Red Snapper
Prawns in Green Curry Paste • Whole Steamed Fish in Yellow
Curry Sauce • Fish Cakes • Steamed Prawns
Steamed Fish in Banana Leaves • Seafood with Egg Noodles
Fried Fish with Tamarind • Sweet Prawn and Coconut Curry

FRIED SPICE FISH

In this recipe a classic Thai sweet-sour chilli sauce is poured over deep-fried fish.

SERVES 2-4

1 large whole fish, eg. red snapper, pomfret or tilapia,
  cleaned and scaled (if necessary)
3 tbsps cornflour
1 tbsp sesame oil
3 large green chillies, seeded and chopped
1 tbsp grated fresh root ginger
2 cloves garlic, crushed
3 tbsps white wine vinegar
2 tbsps fish sauce
90ml/6 tbsps water
2 tbsps palm sugar
6 spring onions, sliced
2 tbsps soy sauce
Oil for frying

Step 1 Cut 3-4 slashes into each side of the fish.

Step 1 Dust with 2 tbsps of the cornflour.

1. Cut 3 or 4 slashes into each side of the fish. Dust with about 2 tbsps of the cornflour. Set aside.

2. Heat the sesame oil in a wok and stir-fry the chillies, ginger and garlic for 2 minutes or until softened.

3. Add the vinegar, fish sauce, water and sugar and simmer gently for 5 minutes. Stir in the spring onions. Mix together the remaining cornflour and soy sauce, add to the pan and cook until slightly thickened. Keep warm.

4. Pour about 5 cm/ 2 inches of oil into a wok or large pan and heat, fry the fish for 5-10 minutes or until cooked through. Place the fish on a serving plate and pour the sauce over the fish.

Cook's Notes

Time
Preparation takes 20 minutes and cooking takes about 20 minutes.

Preparation
The exact cooking time of the fish will depend on its thickness. The flesh will flake easily when it is cooked.

Variation
Small whole fish can be used instead to give each diner their own whole fish.

STIR-FRIED SEAFOOD

Seafood plays a prominent part in Thai cooking,
especially in the southern coastal regions.

SERVES 4

1 tsp black peppercorns
1 shallot, chopped
2 small red chillies, sliced
3 cloves garlic, crushed
2 tbsps oil
225g/8oz peeled raw prawns
340g/12oz prepared mixed seafood, e.g. clams,
    squid, scallops etc.
1 tbsp fish sauce
1 tbsp lime juice
4 spring onions, sliced

1. Place the black peppercorns in a pestle and mortar and crush well. Add the shallot, chillies and garlic and continue to pound until well combined.

Step 1 Crush the peppercorns in a pestle and mortar.

2. Heat the oil in a wok, add the chilli mixture and stir-fry for 1 minute.

3. Add the prawns and the other prepared seafood and stir-fry for 3-4 minutes, or until cooked through.

4. Sprinkle with fish sauce and lime juice. Serve scattered with spring onion slices.

Step 1 Add the shallot, chillies and garlic and continue pounding until well combined.

Step 2 Add the chilli mixture to the oil in a wok and stir-fry for 1 minute.

Cook's Notes

Time
Preparation takes 10 minutes and cooking takes 5-6 minutes.

Cook's Tip
Prepared mixed seafood can be bought in some large supermarkets.

THAI SWEET SOUR FISH

In Thailand, fish is often fried in a wok and served
with a hot sauce, as in this recipe.

SERVES 2

2 x 460g/1lb whole fish such as pomfret, snapper or
   bream, cleaned and scaled (if necessary)
Oil for shallow frying
4 green chillies, seeded and sliced
2.5cm/1-inch piece fresh root ginger, peeled and cut
   into thin sticks
2 cloves garlic, crushed
1 carrot, peeled and cut into thin sticks
3 tbsps white wine vinegar
1 tbsp fish sauce
60g/4 tbsps muscovado sugar
60ml/4 tbsps fish stock
6 spring onions, shredded
1 tsp cornflour mixed with a little water

Step 2 Fry the
chillies, garlic, ginger
and carrot for 3-4
minutes.

Step 4 Stir the
cornflour and water
mixture into the wok
and cook until the
sauce thickens.

Step 1 Cut several
slashes in each side
of the fish.

1. Cut several slashes in each side of the fish. Heat
some oil in a wok or frying pan and fry the fish for 5-10
minutes on each side. Remove the fish from the pan
and keep warm while preparing the sauce.

2. Wipe out the pan and heat a little more oil in it. Fry
the chillies, ginger, garlic and carrot for 3-4 minutes.

3. Stir in the vinegar, fish sauce, sugar and stock and
bring to the boil. Add the spring onions.

4. Stir the cornflour and water mixture into the wok and
cook until the sauce thickens. Pour over the fish to serve.

Cook's Notes

Time
Preparation takes 15 minutes
and cooking takes 20-25 minutes.

Variation
The fish can also be grilled or
barbecued over charcoal.

STEAMED FISH

Steaming is a particularly well suited method of cooking for fish as it does not impair the flavour. The accompanying ingredients added immediately after cooking give this dish a distinct Thai flavour.

SERVES 4

460g/1lb white fish fillets, skinned
2 shallots, sliced
1 stem lemon grass, sliced
3 tbsps lime juice
2 tbsps fish sauce
1 tsp palm sugar
2 cloves garlic, chopped
1 red chilli, chopped
1 green chilli, chopped

1. Cut the fish into thick strips and place in a serving dish that will fit into the top of a steamer.

2. Scatter the sliced shallots and lemon grass over the fish and steam for 10 minutes or until the fish is cooked through.

3. Meanwhile, combine the lime juice, fish sauce and sugar together in a small bowl, stir until the sugar dissolves.

4. Combine the garlic and chillies together in another small bowl.

5. As soon as the fish is cooked, remove from the steamer and pour the fish sauce mixture over it. Scatter the chilli and garlic mixture over the top and serve immediately.

Step 5 As soon as the fish is cooked pour the fish sauce mixture over it.

Step 2 Scatter the sliced shallots and lemon grass over the fish.

Step 5 Scatter the chilli and garlic mixture over the top and serve immediately.

Cook's Notes

Time
Preparation takes 15 minutes and cooking takes about 10 minutes.

Cook's Tip
If wished, the seeds of the chillies can be removed for a milder flavour.

GRILLED RED SNAPPER

Red snapper is a popular fish in Thailand and can be used for many fish dishes. Bream may be used if snapper is unavailable.

SERVES 2

1 large red snapper or bream, cleaned and scaled
1 tbsp Green Curry Paste (see Pastes and
    Dipping Sauces)
140ml/¼ pint thick coconut milk
3 tbsps fish sauce
2 tbsps palm sugar
3 kaffir lime leaves
2 stems lemon grass, sliced
Banana leaf, or baking parchment or foil
Carrot and lemon twigs, to garnish

Step 1 Pour the marinade over the snapper and leave to stand for 1 hour.

1. Cut 3 or 4 slashes into each side of the fish, and place in a dish. Combine the remaining ingredients, except the banana leaf and garnish, and pour over the fish. Allow to marinate for 1 hour.

2. Place the marinated fish on a piece of blanched banana leaf and pour over some of the marinade. Wrap the fish in the banana leaf until completely enclosed and place in a flame-proof dish. Use baking parchment or foil if banana leaves are unavailable.

3. Cook under a preheated medium grill for 25-30 minutes, turning half way through cooking. Alternatively, bake in an oven preheated to 180°C/350°F/Gas Mark

Step 2 Place the marinated fish on a piece of banana leaf, pour over some of the marinade and wrap up.

3, for 30 minutes.

4. Using scissors, cut a large cross in the banana leaf and serve the fish in the banana leaf, garnished with carrot and lemon 'twigs'.

Cook's Notes

Time
Preparation takes 10 minutes, plus 1 hour marinating. Cooking takes 25-30 minutes.

Buying Guide
Buy fish that has bright eyes and firm looking flesh.

PRAWNS IN GREEN CURRY PASTE

This is the hottest of Thai curries because of the large number
of small green Serrano chillies traditionally used in
the Green Curry Paste.

SERVES 2-3

200ml/7fl oz thick coconut milk
2 tbsps Green Curry Paste (see Pastes and
    Dipping Sauces)
340g/12oz peeled, raw prawns
1 tbsp fish sauce
Lemon rind, for garnish

Step 2 Gradually stir
in the remaining
coconut milk.

Step 1 Add the curry
paste to a little of the
coconut milk in a wok
and boil rapidly for 5
minutes, stirring
frequently.

1. Heat a little of the coconut milk in a wok and add the
curry paste. Boil rapidly for 5 minutes, stirring
frequently, then reduce the heat.

2. Gradually stir in the remaining coconut milk and add
the prawns and fish sauce. Cook gently for about 5
minutes until prawns are cooked. Garnish with lemon
rind and serve with steamed rice.

Cook's Notes

 **Time**
Preparation takes 5 minutes and
cooking takes 10 minutes.

 **Serving Idea**
Serve with Thai Steamed Rice.

WHOLE STEAMED FISH IN YELLOW CURRY SAUCE

Steaming is a very popular method of cooking in Thailand.
Here, fish is steamed in a delicious coconut curry sauce.

SERVES 2

2 red mullet, cleaned
1 tbsp oil
1 tbsp Yellow Curry Paste (see Pastes and
    Dipping Sauces)
280ml/½ pint thick coconut milk
2 tbsps fish sauce
2 tbsps light muscovado sugar
2 kaffir lime leaves

Step 3 Stir the remaining coconut milk, fish sauce, sugar and lime leaves into the wok.

1. Cut 3 or 4 slashes on each side of the fish and place in a heat-proof dish which will fit into the top of a steamer.

2. Heat the oil in a wok and fry the curry paste for 1-2 minutes. Stir in half the coconut milk and boil rapidly for 5 minutes.

3. Stir in the remaining coconut milk, fish sauce, sugar and lime leaves.

4. Pour over the fish and steam for 15 minutes or until fish is cooked through. Serve immediately.

Step 4 Pour the sauce over the fish in a heat-proof dish.

Cook's Notes

Time
Preparation takes 15 minutes and cooking takes 25 minutes.

Preparation
The fish will flake easily when it is cooked.

FISH CAKES
(TAUD MAN PLA)

Fish cakes are just one of the delicious savouries that
you can buy from street vendors in Bangkok,
where they make and cook them while you wait.

MAKES 8

275g/10oz white fish fillets, skinned
3 tbsps Red Curry Paste (see Pastes and
   Dipping Sauces)
2 tbsps fish sauce
3 tbsps cornflour
1 tbsp chopped coriander leaves
2 spring onions, finely sliced
1 egg, beaten
Oil for frying
Carrot and spring onion strips, to garnish

Step 1 Place the fish, curry paste, fish sauce, cornflour and coriander in a food processor and process until very finely minced.

1. Place the fish, curry paste, fish sauce, cornflour and coriander in a food processor and process until very finely minced.

2. Remove the mixture from the processor and beat in the spring onions and enough egg to bind the mixture together.

3. Dust hands with flour and shape the mixture into eight small rounds. Chill until required.

4. Shallow- or deep-fry for a few minutes on each side until golden. Garnish with strips of carrot and spring onion.

Step 2 Beat in the spring onions and enough egg to bind the mixture together.

Step 3 Shape the mixture into 8 small cakes using floured hands.

Cook's Notes

Time
Preparation takes 10 minutes and cooking takes 5 minutes.

Serving Idea
Serve with a dipping sauce or chutney of your choice.

STEAMED PRAWNS

Serve these simply prepared prawns with a rice dish such as
Shrimp Paste Fried Rice and a hot dipping sauce.

SERVES 2

460g/1lb raw prawns, in the shell
2 tbsps sesame oil
2 cloves garlic, chopped
2 tbsps chopped fresh coriander root, stem and leaves
2 tsps grated fresh root ginger
1 red chilli, sliced
1 green chilli, sliced
2 tbsps soy sauce
Lemon and lime twists, to garnish

1. Wash and peel the prawns.

2. Combine the remaining ingredients, except the garnish, in a small jug or bowl.

3. Place the prawns in a heat-proof bowl or plate that will fit into a steamer basket. Pour the sauce over

Step 2 Combine the sesame oil, garlic, coriander, ginger, chillies and soy in a small bowl.

Step 3 Pour the sauce over the prawns in a heat-proof bowl.

Step 4 Place the bowl in a steamer, cover and steam for 15 minutes or until the prawns are cooked through.

and toss well.

4. Place the bowl in the steamer, cover and steam for 15 minutes or until the prawns have turned pink and are cooked through.

5. Serve immediately, garnished with lemon and lime twists.

Cook's Notes

Time
Preparation takes 15 minutes and cooking takes about 15 minutes.

Cook's Tip
Do not overcook the prawns as they will become tough.

STEAMED FISH IN BANANA LEAVES (HAW MOK)

Lining the steamer with banana leaves, as they do in Thailand, imparts extra flavour to the dish, but you can use baking parchment or foil instead.

SERVES 4

460g/1lb white fish fillets, skinned
Banana leaves (optional)
2 carrots, peeled and cut into thin sticks
1 red pepper, cut into strips
120g/4oz long beans or French beans, cut into
    7.5cm/3-inch lengths
2 courgettes, cut into thin sticks
140ml/¼ pint thick coconut milk
1-2 tbsps Red Curry Paste (see Pastes and Dipping
    Sauces)
2 kaffir lime leaves
1 tbsp fish sauce

1. Cut the fish into bite-size pieces or strips about 1.25cm/½ inch wide.

2. Line a heat-proof dish, which will fit into your steamer, with banana leaves, baking parchment or foil.

Step 1 Cut the fish into bite-size pieces or strips about 1.25cm/½-inch wide.

Step 2 Line a heat-proof dish, which will fit into your steamer, with banana leaves.

Step 4 Pile the fish pieces on top of the vegetables in the steamer.

3. Blanch the carrots, pepper and beans for 2 minutes in boiling water, add the courgettes for 30 seconds then drain and scatter over the banana leaf.

4. Pile the fish on top of the vegetables.

5. Combine the remaining ingredients and pour over the fish. Cover the steamer and steam for 15-20 minutes or until the fish is cooked through and flakes easily.

Cook's Notes

Time
Preparation takes 15 minutes and cooking takes about 20 minutes.

Cook's Tip
Use a firm-fleshed fish so that it won't break up during cooking.

SEAFOOD WITH EGG NOODLES

Use any mixture of seafood in this spicy dish, which can
be served as a main meal or an impressive side dish.

SERVES 4

460g/1lb mixed seafood, such as prawns, chunks of
    fish, squid, clams and mussels
3 large green chillies, seeded and chopped
1 tbsp chopped fresh coriander leaves
2 cloves garlic, crushed
175g/6oz egg noodles
2 tbsps oil
120g/4oz mange tout peas
120g/4oz baby corn cobs
½ red pepper, sliced
1 tbsp fish sauce
140ml/¼ pint fish stock
1 tbsp lime juice
2 tsps cornflour

Step 2 Pound the
chillies, coriander and
garlic together in a
pestle and mortar.

Step 4 Add the chilli
mixture and the fish
sauce to the
vegetables in the wok
and cook for 2
minutes.

Step 1 If using squid,
score the hoods in a
diamond pattern
before cutting into
pieces.

1. Cook the seafood separately in boiling water until
cooked through, then drain and set aside. If using
squid, score the hoods in a diamond pattern before
cutting into pieces.

2. Pound the chillies, coriander and garlic together in a
pestle and mortar.

3. Cook the noodles as directed on the packet.

4. Heat the oil in a wok, add the mange tout, baby corn
and pepper and stir-fry for 4 minutes. Add the chilli
mixture and fish sauce and cook for 2 minutes.

5. Stir in the fish stock and add the cooked seafood and
noodles to the pan. Mix the lime juice and cornflour
together. Stir into the wok and cook until thickened.

Cook's Notes

Time
Preparation takes 15 minutes
and cooking takes about 15 minutes.

Cook's Tip
Scoring the squid helps to keep it
tender during cooking.

Buying Guide
Mixed prepared seafood can be
bought from large supermarkets.

FRIED FISH WITH TAMARIND
(PLA TOD MAK HAM)

In this dish the fish is served with a delicious sweet and sour sauce.

SERVES 2-4

2 x 460g/1lb whole fish, e.g. red snapper, pomfret or
  bream, cleaned
3 tbsps cornflour
Oil for frying
2 cloves garlic, crushed
1 tbsp grated fresh root ginger
1 small red chilli, sliced
1 small green chilli, sliced
6 spring onions, sliced
1 tbsp soy sauce
2 tbsps palm sugar
2 tbsps fish sauce
140ml/¼ pint tamarind juice
Lemon twists, coriander leaves, sliced spring onion
  tops, to garnish

1. Cut 2-3 slashes on each side of the fish and dredge with the cornflour.

2. Heat about 5cm/2 inches of oil in a wok and fry the fish one at a time for about 5 minutes on each side. When cooked, transfer to a serving dish and keep warm.

3. Carefully pour off most of the oil from the wok and add the garlic, ginger, chillies and spring onions and stir-fry for 2-3 minutes.

4. Stir in the soy sauce, palm sugar and fish sauce and stir until the sugar dissolves.

5. Add the tamarind juice and heat though. Pour some of the sauce over the fish and serve the remainder separately. Garnish with lemon twists, coriander leaves and a pile of spring onion slices.

Step 2 Fry the fish one at a time for about 5 minutes on each side.

Step 3 Stir-fry the garlic, ginger, chillies and spring onions for 2-3 minutes.

Cook's Notes

Time
Preparation takes 15 minutes and cooking takes about 25 minutes.

Buying Guide
If using fish with large scales, make sure they are scraped off before cooking.

Preparation
The exact cooking time for the fish will depend on its thickness. The flesh will flake easily when it is cooked.

SWEET PRAWN AND COCONUT CURRY

This recipe makes a mild curry which is best served with plain Thai Steamed Rice.

SERVES 4

460g/1lb raw prawns, peeled
140ml/¼ pint thick coconut milk
2 tsps lime juice
2 tbsps oil
1 clove garlic, crushed
4 shallots, sliced
1 tbsp grated fresh root ginger
1 tbsp Yellow Curry Paste (see Pastes and Dipping
    Sauces)
5 tsps palm sugar
Lemon and lime wedges and 1 tbsp toasted
    desiccated coconut, to garnish

1. Combine the prawns, coconut milk and lime juice together in a shallow dish. Leave to marinate for at least 30 minutes, stirring occasionally.

2. Heat the oil in a wok and fry the garlic and shallots until softened.

Step 1 Marinate the prawns in the coconut milk and lime juice.

Step 3 Stir the ginger and curry paste into the wok and stir-fry for 1-2 minutes.

Step 4 Add the prawns and their marinade to the wok and cook over a reduced heat for 5 minutes.

3. Stir in the ginger and curry paste and stir-fry for 1-2 minutes. Stir in the sugar.

4. Add the prawns and their marinade to the wok and cook over a reduced heat for 5 minutes or until the prawns turn pink.

5. Transfer to a serving dish and garnish with lemon and lime wedges. Sprinkle with the coconut and serve immediately.

Cook's Notes

Time
Preparation takes 10 minutes, plus at least 30 minutes marinating. Cooking takes about 10 minutes.

Buying Guide
Use ordinary prawns or king prawns for this recipe.

Chapter 3
Meat & Poultry

RED CHICKEN CURRY
(GAENG PED GAI)

Red and green curry pastes are the basis of most Thai curries
and this is a simple one using red curry paste.

SERVES 4

460g/1lb chicken breasts, skinned and boned
2 tbsps oil
2 onions, peeled and cut into wedges
3 tbsps Red Curry Paste (see Pastes and Dipping
 Sauces)
2 kaffir lime leaves, shredded
280ml/½ pint thick coconut milk
120g/4oz canned sliced bamboo shoots (drained
 weight)
1 tbsp fish sauce
2 tbsps sugar

Step 2 Add the curry paste and lime leaves to the wok and fry for a few minutes.

2. Add the curry paste and lime leaves to the wok and fry for a few minutes. Stir in half of the coconut milk and boil rapidly for 3 minutes.

3. Return the chicken to the wok and add the bamboo shoots, fish sauce and sugar. Simmer gently for 5 minutes or until the chicken is cooked. Stir in the remaining coconut milk and cook until heated through.

Step 1 Stir-fry the onion and chicken for 5 minutes or until the onion is softened and beginning to brown.

1. Cut the chicken into bite-size pieces. Heat the oil in a wok and stir-fry the onion and chicken for 5 minutes or until the onion is softened and beginning to brown. Remove from the wok and set aside.

Step 3 Return the chicken to the wok then add the bamboo shoots, fish sauce and sugar. Simmer for 5 minutes or until the chicken is cooked.

Cook's Notes

Time
Preparation takes 15 minutes and cooking takes 15 minutes.

Serving Idea
Accompany with Thai Steamed Rice and Cucumber Salad.

BEEF IN OYSTER SAUCE

You can make this spicy dish very quickly.

SERVES 4

460g/1lb sirloin steak
2 tbsps oil
¼ tsp ground cumin
¼ tsp ground coriander
175g/6oz baby corn
120g/4oz canned bamboo shoots, drained
175g/6oz mange tout peas
2 tbsps oyster sauce
2 tsps dark muscovado sugar
140ml/¼ pint beef stock
1 tsp cornflour
1 tbsp fish sauce
Spring onion slices, to garnish

1. Cut the beef into thin slices and then into strips, using a sharp knife.

2. Heat the oil in a wok and stir-fry the beef over a high

Step 1 Cut the beef into thin slices and then into strips.

Step 2 Fry the beef over a high heat for 5 minutes or until cooked through.

Step 4 Sprinkle with slices of spring onion to garnish.

heat for 5 minutes or until cooked through. Stir in the spices and cook for 1 minute.

3. Add the vegetables, then stir in the oyster sauce, sugar and stock, and bring to the boil.

4. Mix the cornflour with the fish sauce and stir into the pan, cooking until the sauce thickens. Sprinkle with slices of spring onion to garnish.

Cook's Notes

Time
Preparation takes 10 minutes and cooking takes 10 minutes.

Cook's Tip
Partially freezing the beef will make it easier to cut. Slice the meat into strips across the grain to keep it tender.

SPICY MINCED CHICKEN
(LAAB KAI)

This version of a traditional Thai dish comes from the North-East of Thailand, and contains glutinous rice which gives it a delicious nutty texture.

SERVES 4

2 tbsps glutinous rice
2 tbsps oil
2 cloves garlic, crushed
6 small red or green chillies, sliced
340g/12oz chicken, minced
1 tbsp oyster sauce
1 tbsp fish sauce
1 tsp salted black beans
2 tbsps soy sauce
Spring onion slices, to garnish

1. Place the rice in a wok and dry-fry for 5-10 minutes until the grains are golden on all sides, shaking the wok as it cooks.

2. Pour the toasted rice into a pestle and mortar and pound until ground almost to a powder.

3. Heat the oil in the wok and fry the garlic and chillies for 2-3 minutes until softened.

4. Add the chicken and stir-fry, breaking the chicken up as it cooks.

5. Once the chicken is cooked and no longer pink, stir in the oyster sauce, fish sauce, black beans and soy sauce.

6. Add the ground up rice and stir-fry for 2-3 minutes. Serve immediately, scattered with spring onion slices.

Step 1 Dry-fry the rice in a wok for 5-10 minutes until the grains are golden on all sides.

Step 2 Grind the toasted rice in a pestle and mortar until almost a powder.

Step 6 Add the ground up rice to the ingredients in the wok and stir-fry for 2-3 minutes.

Cook's Notes

Time
Preparation takes 15 minutes and cooking takes 25-30 minutes.

Cook's Tip
If you don't have a pestle and mortar, put the rice into a plastic bag and crush with a rolling pin.

PORK CURRY WITH AUBERGINE

This hot and spicy pork curry can be served accompanied
with rice for a delicious meal in itself.

SERVES 6

900g/2lb belly pork slices
2 tbsps oil
3 tbsps Red Curry Paste (see Pastes and Dipping
   Sauces)
570ml/1 pint water
120g/4oz sliced bamboo shoots
6 small white aubergines, quartered
90g/3oz long beans, cut into 2.5cm/1-inch pieces
3 large green chillies, seeded and quartered
   lengthways
2 tbsps fish sauce
1 tbsp lime juice
1 tsp palm sugar
Small bunch sweet basil, torn into pieces

2. Heat the oil in a wok and fry the curry paste for 2-3 minutes, add the meat and fry for 5 minutes.

3. Pour in the water and bring to the boil, then reduce the heat and add the bamboo shoots, aubergines, long beans and chillies. Simmer gently for 10 minutes.

4. Stir in the fish sauce, lime juice, sugar and basil and serve immediately.

Step 2 Add the pork to the curry paste in the wok and fry for 5 minutes.

Step 1 Cut the pork crosswise into 2.5cm/1-inch chunks.

1. Remove the rind from the pork if wished and cut the meat crosswise into 2.5cm/1-inch chunks.

Step 3 Add the bamboo shoots, aubergines, long beans and chillies to the wok and simmer gently for 10 minutes.

Cook's Notes

🕐 **Time**
Preparation takes 20 minutes and cooking takes 25-30 minutes.

👨‍🍳 **Cook's Tip**
Make sure you add the basil at the last moment so that its flavour is preserved.

BARBECUED CHICKEN

These spicy chicken pieces are delicious served with a hot dipping sauce.

SERVES 4-6

680g/1½lbs chicken thighs
2 tbsps Red Curry Paste (see Pastes and Dipping Sauces)
2 cloves garlic, crushed
140ml/¼ pint thick coconut milk
2 tbsps chopped coriander leaves, stem and root

Dipping Sauce
1 small red chilli, sliced
1 small green chilli, sliced
60ml/4 tbsps white wine vinegar

Banana leaves and chilli halves, to garnish

Step 2 Combine the curry paste, garlic, coconut milk and coriander and pour over the chicken in a large dish.

Step 2 Turn the chicken in the marinade and leave to stand for 2 hours.

1. Place the chicken pieces in a large mixing bowl.

2. Combine the curry paste, garlic, coconut milk, and coriander and pour over the chicken. Toss together until all the chicken pieces are well coated. Leave to marinate for 2 hours.

3. Combine the sliced chillies and vinegar to make the dipping sauce, and set aside until required.

4. Cook the chicken pieces over a preheated barbecue or under a preheated grill for 10-15 minutes or until tender. Turn frequently and baste with any remaining marinade during cooking.

5. Serve the chicken hot or cold with the dipping sauce. Garnish with shapes cut from a banana leaf and chilli halves.

Step 3 Combine the sliced chillies and vinegar in a small bowl and set aside until serving time.

Cook's Notes

Time
Preparation takes 10 minutes, plus 2 hours marinating. Cooking takes 10-15 minutes.

Serving Idea
This dish is perfect accompanied with Thai Steamed Rice and Green Papaya Salad.

FIVE-SPICE PORK
(SEE-KRONG MOO OB)

Serve this delicious, sweet, spicy dish with rice.

SERVES 4

680g/1½lbs belly of pork slices
2 tbsps oil
1 tbsp Red Curry Paste (see Pastes and Dipping
   Sauces)
2 tbsps fish sauce
1 tbsp light soy sauce
2 tbsps sugar
1 tsp five-spice powder
1 tbsp chopped lemon grass
Fresh coriander and lime twists, to garnish

Step 2 Stir the fish sauce, soy sauce, sugar, five-spice and lemon grass into the curry paste in the wok. Cook for 3 minutes.

Step 1 Cut the pork strips crosswise into 4cm/1½-inch chunks.

spice powder and lemon grass. Cook for a further 3 minutes.

3. Add the pork to the wok and cook, tossing frequently for 10 minutes or until the pork is cooked through.

4. Serve garnished with fresh coriander and lime twists.

Step 3 Add the pork to the ingredients in the wok and cook, tossing frequently, for 10 minutes.

1. Cut the pork strips into 4cm/1½-inch chunks.

2. Heat the oil in a wok and fry the curry paste for 2 minutes, stir in the fish sauce, soy sauce, sugar, five-

Cook's Notes

Time
Preparation takes 10 minutes and cooking takes 15 minutes.

Preparation
The rind can be taken off the pork if preferred.

BAKED DUCK SALAD

A refreshing salad which makes a delicious meal
in itself, served with steamed rice.

SERVES 4-6

4 duck breasts
1 tsp paprika
312g/11oz can mandarin segments, in natural juice
2 tbsps white wine vinegar
2 tbsps oyster sauce
2 tbsps sesame oil
½ tsp dried chilli flakes
120g/4oz flaked coconut
60g/2oz roasted cashew nuts
Flaked coconut, to garnish

1. Place the duck breasts on a trivet in a roasting dish and sprinkle with the paprika.

2. Roast in an oven preheated to 200°C/400°F/Gas Mark 6, for 35-40 minutes, or until cooked. Allow to cool and cut into thin slices.

Step 3 Drain the juice from the mandarins and combine the vinegar, oyster sauce, oil and chilli flakes.

Step 3 Pour the sauce over the cooked duck and leave to marinate for at least 3 hours.

Step 1 Place the duck breasts on a trivet in a roasting tin and sprinkle the skin with the paprika.

3. Drain the mandarins and reserve the juice. Combine the juice with the vinegar, oyster sauce, oil and chilli flakes. Pour over the sliced duck and leave to marinate for at least 3 hours.

4. Just before serving, toss the coconut and cashew nuts into the duck and marinade. Transfer to a serving dish and arrange the mandarin segments in the centre. Serve garnished with a little extra flaked coconut.

Cook's Notes

Time
Preparation takes 20 minutes plus at least 3 hours marinating. Cooking takes 40 minutes.

Buying Guide
Duck breasts are now available at most large supermarkets.

GREEN CURRY WITH BEEF

Serve this popular Thai curry with rice.

SERVES 4

2 tbsps oil
3 tbsps Green Curry Paste (see Pastes and Dipping
   Sauces)
340g/12oz sirloin or rump steak, sliced
420ml/¾ pint thick coconut milk
2 tbsps fish sauce
4 kaffir lime leaves, torn in half
8 small white aubergines, quartered
2 large red chillies, quartered lengthways
2.5cm/1-inch piece galangal, sliced
1 tsp palm sugar

Step 3 Stir the coconut milk and fish sauce into the wok. Bring to the boil and boil rapidly for 5 minutes.

Step 4 Add the lime leaves, aubergines, chillies, galangal and sugar, to the wok. Simmer for 5-10 minutes.

Step 2 Add the sliced beef to the curry paste in the wok and stir-fry for 2 minutes or until the meat changes colour.

1. Heat the oil in a wok, add the curry paste and fry for 2 minutes, stirring frequently.

2. Add the beef slices and stir-fry for 2 minutes or until

the meat changes colour.

3. Stir in the coconut milk and fish sauce and bring to the boil. Boil rapidly for 5 minutes, stirring occasionally.

4. Reduce the heat and stir in the lime leaves, aubergines, chillies, galangal and sugar. Simmer for 5-10 minutes or until the aubergines are tender.

Cook's Notes

⏰ Time
Preparation takes 15 minutes and cooking takes 20 minutes.

Cook's Tip
Partially freeze the beef to make cutting easier, and slice the meat across the grain to keep it tender.

STIR-FRIED CHICKEN WITH GINGER

This dish appears on many Thai restaurant menus.
It can be served with either rice or noodles.

SERVES 4

2 tbsps oil
2 cloves garlic, crushed
2 shallots, chopped
340g/12oz chicken breast, skinned, boned and cut
    into thin strips
5cm/2-inch piece fresh root ginger, peeled and cut
    into sticks
2 kaffir lime leaves, shredded
60g/2oz whole blanched almonds
120g/4oz long beans, cut into 5cm/2-inch lengths
1 red pepper, cut into strips
90g/3oz water chestnuts, sliced
3 tbsps fish sauce
1 tbsp sugar

1. Heat the oil in a wok and fry the garlic and shallots until beginning to soften. Add the chicken strips and stir-fry until they change colour.

2. Add the ginger, lime leaves, almonds, beans, pepper and water chestnuts.

3. Stir-fry, tossing the ingredients frequently, for 5 minutes or until vegetables are cooked but still crisp. Stir in the fish sauce and sugar and serve.

Step 2 Add the ginger, lime leaves, almonds, beans, pepper and water chestnuts to the wok. Stir-fry for 5 minutes until the vegetables are tender and crisp.

Step 1 Fry the garlic and shallots until beginning to soften.

Step 3 Stir the fish sauce and sugar into the wok.

Cook's Notes

Time
Preparation takes 15 minutes and cooking takes 10 minutes.

Variation
Use unsalted roasted cashew nuts in place of the almonds.

Preparation
Cut the chicken across the grain to keep it tender.

STEAMED PORK CUPS

Served with a light salad and accompanied with a hot dipping sauce
this spicy pork mixture makes an ideal luncheon dish.

SERVES 4-6

460g/1lb lean pork
5 cloves garlic, crushed
6 spring onions, sliced
2 green chillies, sliced
1 tbsp roasted cashew nuts
1 tsp shrimp paste
2 tbsps soy sauce
1 tbsps coriander leaves and stem
Pinch of white pepper
1 tsp palm sugar
120ml/4fl oz thick coconut milk
2 egg whites

Salad
1 red pepper, sliced
1 green pepper, sliced
120g/4oz bean sprouts
2 tbsps lime juice
1 tbsp fish sauce

Step 3 Fold the beaten egg white into the pork mixture using a spatula.

Step 3 Pile the pork mixture into small dishes.

1. Cut the pork into chunks, place in a food processor and process briefly.

2. Add the garlic, spring onions, chillies, cashew nuts, shrimp paste, soy, coriander, pepper and sugar to the processor and process again until all the ingredients are chopped and well combined.

3. Transfer the pork mixture to a bowl and beat in the coconut milk. Whisk the egg whites until standing in soft peaks, then fold into the mixture. Pile the pork mixture into four or six small dishes. Place in a steamer and steam for 20 minutes, or until the mixture is set and cooked through, then remove from the steamer and allow to cool.

4. To make the salad, combine the peppers and bean sprouts and sprinkle with the lime juice and fish sauce.

5. Turn the pork out of the dishes and cut into wedges. Serve with the pepper and bean sprout salad and a hot dipping sauce of your choice (see Pastes and Dipping Sauces).

Cook's Notes

Time
Preparation takes 20 minutes and cooking takes about 20 minutes.

Cook's Tip
Place a sheet of greaseproof paper or foil over the pork as it cooks, to prevent condensation dripping into the dishes.

CHICKEN AND PEANUT CURRY

This dish is sometimes known as dry chicken curry because of its thick sauce.

SERVES 4

460g/1lb chicken breasts, skinned and boned
Juice of 1 lemon
Juice of 1 lime
3 green chillies, seeded and chopped
60ml/4 tbsps oil
1 onion, chopped
¼ tsp ground cumin
¼ tsp ground coriander
120g/4oz roasted peanuts, ground
140ml/¼ pint chicken stock
140ml/¼ pint thick coconut milk
90g/3oz freshly grated coconut flesh
1 tbsp sugar
1 tbsp fish sauce

1. Cut the chicken into bite-size pieces and place in a shallow dish. Mix together the lemon juice, lime juice and chopped chillies and pour over the chicken; toss until all the chicken is coated and leave to marinate for 1 hour.

2. Heat the oil in a wok and fry the onion until softened and beginning to brown. Stir in the cumin and coriander. Remove the chicken from the marinade with a slotted spoon and stir-fry quickly until browned.

3. Add the marinade and cook over a high heat for 2-3 minutes.

4. Stir in the ground roasted peanuts, then gradually add the stock and coconut milk. Add the coconut flesh, sugar and fish sauce, then simmer gently for 5 minutes or until the chicken is cooked through.

Step 2 Remove the chicken from the marinade and add to the ingredients in the wok. Quickly stir-fry the chicken until browned.

Step 3 Add the marinade from the chicken and cook over a high heat for 2-3 minutes.

Step 4 Stir the ground roasted peanuts into the wok.

Cook's Notes

Time
Preparation takes 10 minutes, plus 1 hour marinating. Cooking takes 15 minutes.

Variation
Use crunchy peanut butter instead of ground roasted peanuts.

SPICY MINCED BEEF
(LAAB ISAN)

This hot and spicy dish is a favourite dish in Northern Thailand. If wished, you can remove the seeds from the chillies and reduce their quantity for a milder flavour.

SERVES 4

1 tbsp glutinous rice
1 tbsp oil
1 stem lemon grass, sliced
4 small red chillies, sliced
2 cloves garlic, chopped
1 tbsp grated fresh root ginger
460g/1lb lean minced beef
Juice of 1 lemon
2 tbsps fish sauce
1 tbsp chopped coriander leaves
Lime wedges, to garnish

Step 2 Pound the toasted rice in pestle and mortar, until it is almost ground to a powder.

Step 4 Add the beef to the wok and cook until it changes colour, breaking it up as it cooks.

Step 1 Dry-fry the rice in a wok for 5-10 minutes or until golden on all sides.

1. Place the rice in a wok and dry-fry for 5-10 minutes until the grains are golden on all sides, shaking the wok as it cooks.

2. Pour the toasted rice into a pestle and mortar and pound until ground almost to a powder.

3. Heat the oil in the wok and stir-fry the lemon grass, chillies, garlic and ginger for 3 minutes.

4. Add the beef and cook until the meat changes colour, breaking it up as it cooks.

5. When the meat is cooked, sprinkle with lemon juice and fish sauce. Stir in the ground rice and cook for 1 minute.

6. Transfer to a serving dish, scatter with the chopped coriander leaves, and garnish with lime wedges.

Cook's Notes

Time
Preparation takes 15 minutes and cooking takes 15-20 minutes.

Preparation
If you don't have a pestle and mortar, put the toasted rice in a plastic bag and crush with a rolling pin.

YELLOW CHICKEN CURRY
(KAENG KARRI KAI)

This easy-to-prepare curry illustrates the Indian
influence on traditional Thai cuisine.

SERVES 4

460g/1lb chicken breast, skinned and boned
2 tbsps oil
2 cloves garlic, sliced
1 onion, peeled and cut into wedges
3 tbsps Yellow Curry Paste, (see Pastes and
  Dipping Sauces)
570ml/1 pint thick coconut milk
1 small potato, peeled and cut into chunks
2 kaffir lime leaves, shredded

1. Cut the chicken into even-sized chunks.

2. Heat the oil in a wok and fry the garlic and onion for
3 minutes, then stir in the curry paste and fry for 1
minute.

3. Stir in half the coconut milk and bring to the boil. Boil
rapidly for 5 minutes, stirring occasionally. Stir in the

Step 2 Fry the garlic
and onion for 3
minutes then stir in
the curry paste and
fry for 1 minute.

Step 3 Stir in half the
coconut milk and boil
for 5 minutes, stirring
occasionally.

Step 3 Stir in the
remaining coconut
milk and bring to the
boil.

remaining coconut milk, bring to the boil and add the
potatoes and chicken.

4. Reduce the heat and simmer gently for 20-30
minutes or until the chicken is cooked and the potato is
tender.

5. Spoon into serving dishes and sprinkle with the lime
leaves.

Cook's Notes

Time
Preparation takes 10 minutes
and cooking takes 30-40 minutes.

Serving Idea
Accompany with Thai Steamed
Rice or Stir-Fried Thai Noodles.

BARBECUED PORK

Traditionally this dish would be cooked on charcoal burners
by the roadside, but it works just as well in the oven.

SERVES 4

4 cloves garlic, crushed
140ml/¼ pint light soy sauce
60g/2oz dark muscovado sugar
1 tbsp grated fresh root ginger
1 tbsp chopped fresh coriander stems and root
4 whole star anise or 1 tsp ground anise
Red food colouring (optional)
2 pork fillets
2 tbsps oil
2 shallots, chopped
120g/4oz ground roasted peanuts
140ml/¼ pint pork or chicken stock
1 tsp cornflour mixed with a little water
Lime leaves and star anise, to garnish

1. Mix together the garlic, soy, sugar, ginger, coriander, anise and a few drops of food colouring, if wished, to make a marinade.

2. Place the pork fillets in a shallow dish and add the marinade. Turn the pork over so that it is fully coated and leave to marinate for at least 1 hour, turning once.

3. Remove the meat from the marinade and place on a trivet in a roasting tin. Roast in an oven preheated to 375°F/190°C/Gas Mark 5, for 20 minutes or until pork is cooked. Baste once or twice with some of the marinade during cooking. Test the pork with a skewer – the juices should run clear.

4. Just before the end of the roasting time, heat the oil in a wok and fry the shallots until tender and beginning to brown. Stir in the ground peanuts, the remaining marinade and the stock. Cook until simmering, then stir in the cornflour mixture and cook a

Step 1 Mix together the garlic, soy, sugar, ginger, coriander, anise and food colouring.

Step 2 Add the pork to the marinade, turn it so that it is completely coated and leave to marinate for at least 1 hour.

Step 3 Test the pork with a skewer, if it is cooked the juices will run clear.

little longer until thickened.

5. To serve, slice the pork and pour the sauce over. Garnish with lime leaves and star anise.

Cook's Notes

Time
Preparation takes 15 minutes plus 1 hour marinating. Cooking takes 20 minutes.

Preparation
The pork can be cooked on a barbecue if wished.

CHICKEN WITH CHILLI AND BASIL

Three kinds of basil are used in Thailand, but Bai Horapa is the nearest to European basil. Look out for the other Thai varieties in Asian shops.

SERVES 4

4 chicken quarters
3 large red chillies, seeded and chopped
1 tbsp fresh coriander root and stem, chopped
2 cloves garlic, crushed
3 tbsps oil
2 green chillies, sliced
2 tbsps fish sauce
1 tbsp oyster sauce (optional)
Small bunch basil, torn into small pieces
Chilli 'flowers', to garnish

and almost cooked through. Remove from the pan.

4. Add the pounded chilli mixture and fry for a few minutes. Return the chicken to the pan and add the green chillies, fish sauce and oyster sauce if using. Cook over a medium heat for 5-10 minutes or until chicken is completely cooked.

5. Stir in the basil leaves and serve garnished with chilli 'flowers'.

Step 1 Cut the chicken quarters into smaller pieces using a large sharp knife or a cleaver.

Step 3 Fry the chicken pieces until golden and almost cooked through.

Step 4 Add the green chillies to the chicken in the wok.

1. Cut the chicken into smaller pieces using a large sharp knife or a meat cleaver.

2. Pound the red chillies, coriander and garlic together in a pestle and mortar.

3. Heat the oil in a wok and fry the chicken until golden

Cook's Notes

Time
Preparation takes 20 minutes and cooking takes 20 minutes.

Cook's Tip
Tearing basil leaves rather than cutting them with a knife allows more flavour to be released.

MUSSAMAN CURRY

This curry illustrates the Indian influence on some of Thailand's cuisine.

SERVES 4

4 cardamom pods
½ tsp coriander seeds
½ tsp caraway seeds
2 whole cloves
5 small red chillies, chopped
1 clove garlic, crushed
1 stem lemon grass, roughly chopped
2 spring onions, chopped
¼ tsp grated root ginger
¼ tsp ground nutmeg
1 tbsp oil
Oil for shallow frying
340g/12oz potatoes, peeled and cut into chunks
2-3 onions, peeled and cut into wedges
675g/1½lbs sirloin steak, cut into bite-size chunks
420ml/¾ pint thin coconut milk
2 tbsps dark muscovado sugar
1 tsp tamarind juice
Chopped coriander, to garnish

Step 1 Crush the cardamom pods with the side of a knife and remove the seeds.

Step 2 Dry-fry the spices in a wok for 1 minute.

1. Crush the cardamom pods with the side of a knife and remove the seeds.

2. Place the coriander seeds, caraway seeds, cardamom and cloves in a wok and dry-fry for 1 minute, tossing frequently to prevent burning. Remove from the heat.

3. Mix the fried seeds, chillies, garlic, lemon grass, spring onions, ginger, nutmeg and oil together and pound in a pestle and mortar.

4. Heat the oil for shallow frying in a wok and fry the potato and onion wedges for 5 minutes or until they

begin to soften, then remove and set aside.

5. Add the meat to the pan and fry until browned. Stir in a quarter of the coconut milk and simmer gently for 30 minutes or until meat is very tender.

6. Remove the meat from the wok with a slotted spoon and set aside. Add the chilli mixture to the wok and boil rapidly for 5 minutes, then blend in the remaining milk.

7. Return the meat, onions and potatoes to the wok. Stir in the sugar and tamarind juice and cook gently for 20 minutes. Garnish with chopped coriander.

Cook's Notes

🕐 **Time**
Preparation takes 25 minutes and cooking takes 1 hour.

👨‍🍳 **Cook's Tip**
Cut the steak across the grain to keep it tender.

Chapter 4

Pastes &
Dipping
Sauces

GREEN AND RED CURRY PASTES

Red and green curry pastes are the basis of most Thai curries.
Red curry paste is milder than the green.
MAKES 45-60ML/3-4 TBSPS OF EACH

Green Curry Paste
16 green Serrano or other small chillies, chopped
3 cloves garlic, crushed
2 stems lemon grass, roughly chopped
3 spring onions, chopped
1 tsp grated fresh root ginger
1 tsp coriander seeds
1 tsp caraway seeds
4 whole cloves
1 tsp ground nutmeg
1 tsp shrimp paste
3 tbsps oil

Red Curry Paste
12 small red chillies, chopped
3 cloves garlic, crushed
1 stem lemon grass, chopped
1 small onion, finely chopped
1 tsp grated fresh root ginger
2 tsps chopped coriander stems and root
Large pinch of cumin
1 tsp shrimp paste
2 tbsps oil

1. To make either the red or green curry paste, place the chillies, garlic, lemon grass and onion in a pestle and mortar and pound until the mixture is well bruised and the juices begin to blend.

2. Add all the remaining ingredients except the oil and continue to pound until a paste is formed. Finally blend in the oil.

3. The curry pastes can also be made in a mini food processor (the quantity is too small for a full size blender or processor). Place all the ingredients in the processor and grind to a paste.

Step 2 Blend the oil into the ingredients in the pestle and mortar.

 Time
Preparation takes 15 minutes for each paste.

Cook's Tip
The pastes will keep for up to 1 month in the refrigerator.

Preparation
Store the paste in an airtight jar and refrigerate until required.

YELLOW CURRY PASTE

The turmeric in this paste gives curries a lovely golden hue.
It has less heat than either the red or the green curry pastes.

MAKES 75-90ML/5-6 TBSPS

2 tbsps cumin seeds
2 tbsps coriander seeds
3 stems lemon grass, chopped
1 tbsp grated fresh root ginger
6 red chillies, seeded and chopped
1 tsp salt
3 cloves garlic, crushed
1 small shallot, finely chopped
1 tsp ground turmeric
1 tsp shrimp paste

1. Place the cumin and coriander seeds in a wok without any oil and dry-fry for 3-4 minutes, shaking the wok frequently to prevent the spices from burning. Remove from the heat and set aside.

2. Place the lemon grass and ginger in a large pestle and mortar and pound together until well crushed. Add the chillies and salt and continue pounding together for about 4 minutes.

3. Add the garlic and shallot and pound until broken down, then add the fried spices and turmeric. Finally, add the shrimp paste and continue to pound together until a smooth moist paste is produced.

NAM PRIK

This is a hot dipping sauce which can be served with most Thai dishes,
but is particularly good served with relatively mild dishes.

SERVES 4

1 tsp shrimp paste
1 tsp salt
1 tsp light muscovado sugar
4 cloves garlic, crushed
5 small red chillies, chopped
8 anchovy fillets, chopped
½ tbsp light soy sauce
Juice of ½ lime

1. Pound together the shrimp paste, salt, sugar, garlic, chillies and anchovies to a smooth paste in a pestle and mortar or mini food processor.

2. Stir in the soy sauce and lime juice and transfer to a small serving dish.

Cook's Notes

Time
Yellow Curry Paste: preparation takes 15 minutes.
Nam Prik: Preparation takes 10 minutes.

Cook's Tip
Yellow Curry Paste: store the paste in an airtight jar in the refrigerator until required. The paste will keep for up to 1 month.

Serving Idea
Nam Prik: serve with Pork Wrapped in Noodles or Mixed Vegetable Stir-Fry.

SWEET CHILLI SAUCE

A delicious tangy sweet and sour chilli sauce.

SERVES 4

120g/4oz canned plums (drained weight), pitted
1 tbsp oil
3 red chillies, chopped
1 clove garlic, crushed
1 tsp palm sugar
2 tbsps white wine vinegar
Fish sauce, to taste

1. Chop the plums very finely, this can be done in a food processor if wished.

2. Heat the oil in a small pan or wok and fry the chillies and garlic for 3 minutes, until just softened. Stir in the remaining ingredients and heat through.

SWEET AND SOUR DIPPING SAUCE

Another popular dipping sauce that
can be served with a lot of Thai dishes.

SERVES 4

60g/2oz cucumber
30g/1oz carrots, peeled
140ml/¼ pint white wine vinegar
60g/2oz palm sugar
1 tsp chopped fresh coriander

1. Cut the cucumber and carrots into very small dice.

2. Combine with all the other ingredients in a bowl and stir until the sugar dissolves.

Cook's Notes

Time
Preparation takes 10 minutes for each sauce.

Serving Idea
Sweet Chilli Sauce: serve with Thai Spring Rolls or other similar dishes.

Cook's Tip
Sweet and Sour Dipping Sauce: this sauce is best served freshly made.

FISH SAUCE WITH CHILLI

As well as being used as a dipping sauce, this can be used in curries
and stir-fries to add spiciness and saltiness to the dish.

SERVES 4

60ml/4 tbsps fish sauce
1 tbsp lime juice
½ tsp palm sugar
6 small green chillies, sliced into circles
½ small shallot, finely chopped

1. Combine the fish sauce and lime juice together in a small bowl. Add the sugar and stir until dissolved.

2. Add the prepared chillies and shallot and stir until well combined; leave to stand for at least 30 minutes before using.

NUOC CHAM

This sauce is delicious served with rice or Spicy Prawn Wraps.

SERVES 4

1 tbsp lime juice
60ml/4 tbsps fish sauce
3 tbsps water
1 tsp palm sugar
1 red chilli, seeded and shredded
1 tbsp grated carrot
1 tbsp chopped roasted peanuts

1. Combine the lime juice, fish sauce and water in a small bowl and add the sugar. Stir until the sugar dissolves.

2. Add the chilli and grated carrot, then stir in the roasted peanuts.

Cook's Notes

Time
Fish Sauce with Chilli: preparation takes 5 minutes, plus 30 minutes standing before using. Nuoc Cham: preparation takes 10 minutes.

Serving Idea
Fish Sauce with Chilli: serve as a dipping sauce or over rice.

Cook's Tip
Nuoc Cham: this sauce is best served freshly made.

Chapter 5
Rice, Noodles & Vegetables

THAI STEAMED RICE

Thai jasmine rice is a fragrant rice with a delicate flavour. Do not add salt during cooking as this will destroy the slightly nutty flavour.

SERVES 4-6

225g/8oz jasmine rice
570ml/1 pint water

1. Rinse the rice under running water and drain.

2. Place the rice and the measured water in a saucepan and bring gently to the boil.

Step 3 Cook the rice gently with the measured water for 10 minutes or until the water has been absorbed.

3. Stir the rice, cover, reduce the heat and simmer gently for 10 minutes or until the water has been absorbed.

4. Line a steamer with a piece of muslin and pile the rice into the steamer. Steam over gently simmering water for 30 minutes.

5. Leave the rice to stand for a few minutes, then fluff up gently with a fork.

Step 4 Line a steamer with a piece of muslin.

Step 4 Pile the rice into the steamer and cook over gently simmering water for 30 minutes.

Cook's Notes

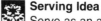

Time
Preparation takes 5 minutes and cooking takes about 40 minutes.

Serving Idea
Serve as an accompaniment to a Thai curry.

BAKED PINEAPPLE RICE
(KHAO OP SAPPAROD)

This attractively presented rice dish is from Bangkok and the Central Plains.

SERVES 6

1 pineapple
2 tbsps oil
1 clove garlic, crushed
4 shallots, chopped
1 tbsp Yellow Curry Paste (see Pastes and
    Dipping Sauces)
460g/1lb cooked rice
140ml/¼ pint thick coconut milk
60g/2oz raisins
60g/2oz toasted cashew nuts
Chilli 'flowers', to garnish

Step 1 Cut the pineapple in half and scoop out the flesh to leave two shells with a thin border of flesh attached.

1. Cut the pineapple in half lengthwise, keeping the leaves attached. Scoop out the flesh using a tablespoon and a paring knife, to leave two shells with a thin border of flesh attached. Chop half the flesh to use later in the dish; the remaining pineapple is not needed for this recipe.

2. Heat the oil in a wok and fry the garlic and shallots

Step 4 Pile the rice mixture into the pineapple shells.

Step 4 Wrap the pineapple laves in foil to prevent them from burning.

until softened. Stir in the curry paste and fry for 1 minute.

3. Add the rice and toss together with the shallot mixture. Stir in the coconut milk, raisins, chopped pineapple and cashew nuts.

4. Pile the rice mixture into the pineapple shells. Wrap the pineapple leaves in foil to prevent them from burning and place on a baking sheet.

5. Bake in an oven preheated to 170°C/325°F/Gas Mark 3, for 20 minutes. Remove from the foil and serve garnished with chilli 'flowers'.

Cook's Notes

Time
Preparation takes 20 minutes and cooking takes about 25 minutes.

Cook's Tip
If the pineapple shells won't stand stable, cut a thin slice from the base.

THAI FRIED RICE (KHAO PAD)

Add different fresh vegetables to the rice according
to what you have to hand.

SERVES 4-6

A little oil
1 egg, beaten
1 tbsp thin coconut milk
120g/4oz chicken breasts, skinned and cut into small
 pieces
120g/4oz raw, peeled prawns
1 small red or green chilli, seeded and chopped
1 tbsp Red or Green Curry Paste (see Pastes and
 Dipping Sauces)
2 tbsps fish sauce
680g/1½lbs cooked rice
120g/4oz long beans, cut into 2.5cm/1-inch lengths
6 spring onions, sliced diagonally
Chilli 'flowers', to garnish

1. Heat a wok and brush with a little oil. Beat together
the egg and coconut milk and pour into the wok. Swirl
wok so that the egg coats it, to form a thin omelette.

2. Cook for a minute until just brown on the underside
then flip over and cook the other side.

3. Remove from the wok and allow to cool slightly. Roll
up and cut into thin strips; set aside.

4. Heat a little more oil in the wok and add the chicken
and prawns. Cook quickly, stirring frequently.

5. Add the chilli, curry paste and fish sauce to the pan
and heat until sizzling hot. Stir in the rice, beans and
spring onions.

6. Reduce the heat slightly and cook, stirring
constantly, until the rice is hot.

Step 1 Pour the egg
and coconut mixture
into the hot wok and
swirl so that it coats
the wok and forms a
thin omelette.

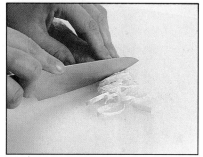

Step 3 Shred the
rolled up omelette
into thin strips.

Step 7 Garnish the
rice with the
shredded omelette
and chilli 'flowers'.

7. Pile into a serving dish and garnish with the
shredded omelette and chilli 'flowers'.

Cook's Notes

Time
Preparation takes 15 minutes
and cooking takes 15 minutes.

Cook's Tip
Before using the cooked rice,
cool it by spreading out on a clean
tea-towel which will also absorb all the
excess moisture.

THAI RICE SALAD (KHAO YAM)

A delicious and attractive salad from southern Thailand.

SERVES 4

340g/12oz cooked rice
½ cucumber
1 grapefruit
6 spring onions
2.5cm/1-inch piece fresh root ginger
60g/2oz shredded coconut
60g/2oz bean sprouts
60g/2oz dried shrimps, chopped
2 stems lemon grass, thinly sliced

Sauce
120ml/4 fl oz fish sauce
60ml/4 tbsps lime juice
2 tbsps light muscovado sugar

1. Divide the rice into four and press a quarter of the rice into a ramekin dish or tea cup. Turn out onto an individual serving plate. Repeat with the remaining rice.

Step 1 Turn the rice out onto an individual serving plates.

Step 4 Each diner should scatter the individual salad ingredients over their portion of rice.

2. Cut the cucumber into quarters and slice thinly. Cut off all the peel and pith of the grapefruit and segment the flesh. Slice the spring onions diagonally. Peel the ginger and cut into thin sticks.

3. Arrange the different salad ingredients separately on a serving platter. Combine the ingredients for the sauce and pour into one large or four small dishes.

4. Each diner should scatter some of the individual ingredients over their mound of rice and then drizzle the sauce over the top.

Step 4 The sauce is drizzled over just before eating.

Cook's Notes

 Time
Preparation takes 20 minutes.

Variation
The salad ingredients can be mixed together and tossed in the sauce just before serving.

FRIED RICE WITH CRAB
(KHAO PAD POO)

For fried rice dishes such as this use chilled,
cooked rice as it will break up more readily.

SERVES 4

2 tbsps oil
2 eggs, beaten
2 shallots, chopped
2 cloves garlic, crushed
680g/1½lbs cooked rice
2 small red chillies, sliced
170g/6oz can crabmeat, drained
2 tbsps fish sauce
Lime wedges, to garnish

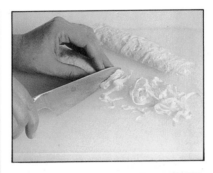

Step 2 Slice the rolled up omelettes into thin shreds.

Step 1 Add half the egg to the wok and swirl thinly to coat and form a thin omelette.

Step 3 Add the cooked rice to the wok and stir-fry for 2 minutes.

1. Heat 1 tbsp of the oil in a wok and add about half the egg. Swirl to thinly coat the wok and form a thin omelette. Cook until the egg sets then remove from the wok. Repeat with the remaining egg.

2. Roll up each omelette, shred thinly and set aside.

3. Heat the remaining oil in the wok and fry the shallots and garlic until softened. Add the rice and fry, stirring frequently, for 2 minutes.

4. Stir in the chillies, crab and fish sauce and stir-fry for 2-3 minutes or until the rice and crab are piping hot.

5. Toss in the egg strips and serve garnished with lime wedges.

Cook's Notes

Time
Preparation takes 10 minutes and cooking takes 10 minutes.

Serving Idea
Serve accompanied with a dipping sauce such as Fish Sauce with Chilli.

SHRIMP PASTE FRIED RICE
(KHAO CLOOK GAPI)

This is a strongly flavoured rice dish which is
best served with steamed vegetables.

SERVES 4

2 tbsps oil
30g/1oz dried shrimps
4 cloves garlic, crushed
2 red chillies, seeded and chopped
680g/1½lbs cooked rice
2 tbsps shrimp paste
2 eggs, beaten
4 spring onions, sliced
3 tbsps fish sauce
Coriander leaves, to garnish

1. Heat the oil in a wok and fry the dried shrimps for about 30 seconds, remove and set aside to drain on kitchen paper.

2. Add the garlic and chillies and fry until softened.

3. Stir in the rice and shrimp paste and stir-fry for 5 minutes or until heated through.

4. Add the beaten eggs and spring onions and cook over a low heat, stirring until the egg is cooked. Add the fish sauce.

5. To serve, sprinkle with the fried dried shrimps and garnish with coriander leaves.

Step 4 Add the beaten egg and spring onions to the rice. Cook over a low heat, stirring until the egg is cooked.

Step 1 Fry the dried shrimps for about 30 seconds.

Step 5 Sprinkle with the fried dried shrimps to serve.

Cook's Notes

Time
Preparation takes 10 minutes and cooking takes 15 minutes.

Serving Idea
Serve with vegetables such as steamed bok choy or long beans.

SPICY RICE WITH CHICKEN

This spicy rice dish can also be served as a light lunch or supper dish.

SERVES 4

225g/8oz cooked chicken
120g/4oz long beans, cut into 2.5cm/1-inch lengths
1 tbsp oil
2 tbsps Red Curry Paste (see Pastes and
    Dipping Sauces)
460g/1lb cooked rice
2 tbsps fish sauce
1 tsp palm sugar
Chilli 'flowers' and spring onions, to garnish

1. Cut the chicken into thin shreds. Blanch the beans in boiling water for 5 minutes or until just tender.

2. Heat the oil in a wok and fry the curry paste for 3-4 minutes, stirring frequently.

3. Add the chicken and rice to the wok and stir-fry for 5

Step 1 Cut the cooked chicken into thin shreds using a sharp knife.

Step 2 Fry the curry paste for 3-4 minutes stirring frequently.

minutes, tossing frequently.

4. Add the beans and cook a further 2 minutes or until all the ingredients are piping hot.

5. Mix together the fish sauce and sugar, stir until the sugar dissolves. Add to the wok. Toss well and serve garnished with chilli 'flowers' and spring onions.

Step 4 Add the blanched beans to the ingredients in the wok and cook for 2 minutes, or until all the ingredients are hot.

Cook's Notes

Time
Preparation takes 10 minutes and cooking takes 15 minutes.

Variation
Use cooked pork instead of the chicken and substitute oyster sauce for the fish sauce.

STIR-FRIED THAI NOODLES
(PAD THAI)

This is a well-known basic Thai dish with as many
variations as there are Thai cooks.

SERVES 4

175g/6oz rice noodles
60ml/4 tbsps oil
225g/8oz tofu, cut into cubes
3 cloves garlic, crushed
60g/2oz dried shrimps
3 tbsps chopped pickled turnip
60ml/4 tbsps fish sauce
30g/1oz palm sugar
1 tbsp soy sauce
2 tbsps tamarind juice
2 eggs, beaten
1 tbsp chopped garlic chives
60g/2oz roasted peanuts, chopped
225g/8oz bean sprouts
Chilli strips, to garnish

Step 1 Soak the rice noodles in boiling water for 10-15 minutes or until softened.

1. Soak the rice noodles in boiling water for 10-15 minutes or until softened, then drain and set aside.

2. Heat the oil in a wok and fry the tofu cubes until browned on all sides. Remove with a slotted spoon and set aside.

Step 2 Fry the tofu cubes in a wok until browned on all sides.

3. Add the garlic and dried shrimps to the wok and stir-fry for 2 minutes. Reduce the heat and add the noodles. Cook for 5 minutes, tossing the ingredients frequently. Add the pickled turnip, fish sauce, sugar, soy and tamarind juice and cook for 2 minutes.

4. Add the beaten egg and cook, tossing the ingredients together until the egg sets. Stir in the tofu, garlic chives, peanuts and beans sprouts. Garnish with chilli strips and serve immediately.

Step 3 Add the noodles to the ingredients in the wok and cook for 5 minutes, tossing the ingredients frequently.

Cook's Notes

Time
Preparation takes 10 minutes, plus 10-15 minutes soaking. Cooking takes about 15 minutes.

Variation
Cashew nuts may be used instead of peanuts and sliced bamboo shoots instead of bean sprouts.

STIR-FRIED GLASS NOODLES WITH CHICKEN

Serve as part of a Thai meal or as a light supper snack for 2-3 people.

SERVES 4

1 chicken breast, skinned and boned
2 tbsps oyster sauce
2 tbsps fish sauce
1 tbsp soy sauce
1 tsp palm sugar
½ large red chilli, seeded and chopped
½ tsp grated fresh root ginger
175g/6oz cellophane noodles
2 tbsps oil
2 cloves garlic, crushed
1 red onion, sliced
Coriander leaves, to garnish

Step 3 Add the chicken and the marinade to the garlic and onion in a wok and stir-fry for about 10 minutes or until the chicken is cooked through.

Step 4 Add the drained noodles to the wok and toss over a low heat until heated through.

Step 1 Marinate the chicken slices in the oyster sauce, fish sauce, soy, sugar, chilli and ginger.

1. Cut the chicken into thin slices. Combine the oyster sauce, fish sauce, soy, sugar, chilli and ginger in a shallow dish. Add the chicken and toss until well coated. Leave to marinate for 20 minutes.

2. Soak the noodles in boiling water for 5 minutes, until softened. Drain and set aside.

3. Heat the oil in a wok and fry the garlic and onion until just softened. Add the chicken and the marinade and stir-fry for about 10 minutes or until the chicken is cooked through.

4. Add the noodles to the wok and toss over a low heat until heated through. Pile onto a serving dish and garnish with coriander leaves.

Cook's Notes

Time
Preparation takes 5 minutes plus 20 minutes marinating. Cooking takes about 15 minutes.

Cook's Tip
Partially freeze the chicken to make slicing easier. Cut the chicken across the grain to keep the meat tender.

SPICY STEAMED PORK WITH NOODLES

In Thailand noodle dishes like this are served as part of the main course or as a snack at any time of the day.

SERVES 4

225g/8oz minced pork
1 tsp ground coriander
1 tsp ground cumin
1 tsp ground turmeric
1 bunch bok choy or spinach, washed
1-2 tbsps Red or Green Curry Paste (see Pastes and Dipping Sauces)
1 tsp shrimp paste
140ml/¼ pint thick coconut milk
175g/6oz egg noodles
Chopped fresh coriander, to garnish

1. Place the minced pork and ground spices in a food processor and process until very finely chopped. Shape the pork mixture into small balls using dampened hands.

2. Tear the bok choy into large pieces and place in a heat-proof dish that will fit into a steamer. Arrange the meat balls on top.

3. Mix together the curry paste, shrimp paste and coconut milk and pour over the meat balls. Cover and steam for 20 minutes.

4. Meanwhile, cook the noodles as directed on the packet. Mix the noodles together with the pork and bok choy or arrange noodles on a plate and pile the pork mixture on top. Garnish with a sprinkling of chopped coriander leaves.

Step 2 Tear the bok choy into large pieces and place in a heatproof dish that will fit into a steamer.

Step 3 Pour the curry paste, shrimp paste and coconut milk mixture over the meat balls in the steamer. Cover and steam for 20 minutes.

Step 4 While the meat balls are cooking, cook the noodles as directed on the packet.

Cook's Notes

Time
Preparation takes 20 minutes and cooking takes 20 minutes.

Preparation
The pork can be mixed with the spices by hand. Add a little beaten egg if necessary, to help bind the mixture together.

TOFU WITH CRISPY NOODLES

Tofu is ideal for making vegetarian main courses as it
can be used to replace meat or fish.

SERVES 4

Oil for deep-frying
120g/4oz rice noodles (vermicelli)
225g/8oz tofu, drained and patted dry
2 carrots, peeled and sliced
90g/3oz broccoli florets
2 sticks celery, sliced
1 onion, peeled and cut into wedges
1 tsp shrimp paste
2 tbsps light soy sauce
3 tbsps white wine vinegar
2 tbsps dark muscovado sugar
1 tsp grated fresh root ginger

1. Heat the oil to 180°C/360°F in a wok. Add the rice noodles in small batches, turn over and fry for a few seconds. The rice will puff up immediately.

2. Remove from the oil and drain well on kitchen paper.

Step 1 Add the rice noodles in small batches to the hot oil in the wok.

3. Cut the tofu into cubes and fry for a few minutes until browned on all sides, remove from the oil and set aside.

4. Pour off most of the oil, add the carrots, broccoli, celery and onion to the wok and stir-fry for 2 minutes or until the vegetables are cooked but still crisp.

5. Stir in the shrimp paste, soy sauce, vinegar, sugar and ginger. Return the vermicelli and tofu to the wok, toss to mix and serve immediately.

Step 2 As soon as the rice has puffed up remove it from the oil and drain on kitchen paper.

Step 3 Fry the cubed tofu for a few minutes until browned on all sides, then remove from the oil and drain well.

Cook's Notes

Time
Preparation takes 10 minutes and cooking takes 10 minutes.

Variation
Use smoked tofu for more flavour.

CHAING MAI NOODLES (KHAO SOI)

Originally from Burma, this dish has evolved to have a distinct Thai flavour.

SERVES 4-6

2 tbsps oil
2 cloves garlic, crushed
4 shallots, chopped
1 tbsp Red Curry Paste (see Pastes and
   Dipping Sauces)
½ tsp ground turmeric
Pinch of ground cumin
Pinch of ground coriander
280ml/½ pint coconut milk
225g/8oz rump or sirloin steak, thinly sliced
75ml/5 tbsps fish sauce
60g/2oz palm sugar
1 tbsp soy sauce
2 tbsps lime juice
1 tbsp garlic chives, chopped
460g/1lb fresh egg noodles
Chilli 'flowers' and crispy egg noodles (optional),
   to garnish

1. Heat the oil in a wok and fry the garlic and shallots until softened.

2. Stir in the curry paste, turmeric, cumin and coriander. Stir-fry for 1 minute.

3. Add the coconut milk and bring to the boil, reduce the heat and add the beef. Simmer for 15-20 minutes or

Step 3 Add the beef to the ingredients in the wok and simmer for 10-15 minutes or until the beef is tender.

until the beef is cooked.

4. Stir in the fish sauce, sugar, soy, lime juice and garlic chives.

5. Meanwhile, cook the egg noodles in boiling water for 1 minute. Drain and arrange on a serving dish. Spoon the beef on top and serve garnished with chilli 'flowers' and crispy noodles if wished.

Step 5 While the beef is cooking, cook the fresh egg noodles in boiling water for 1 minute.

Cook's Notes

Time
Preparation takes 20 minutes and cooking takes about 20 minutes.

Cook's Tip
Cut the steak across the grain to keep it tender.

Preparation
To make the noodle garnish, deep-fry a few of the cooked egg noodles until crispy.

STIR-FRIED BABY CORN WITH MUSHROOMS

Serve this tasty vegetable dish as part of a complete Thai meal.

SERVES 4

2 tbsps oil
2 cloves garlic, crushed
4 shallots, chopped
460g/1lb baby corn, cut in half lengthways
120g/4oz mange tout peas
225g/8oz can straw mushrooms (drained weight)
1 tbsp grated galangal
½ tsp dried chilli flakes
1 tbsp fish sauce
1 tbsp soy sauce

1. Heat the oil in a wok and fry the garlic and shallots until softened.

Step 1 Fry the garlic and shallots in the oil until softened.

Step 2 Stir in the baby corn and cook for 5 minutes, then add the mange tout peas and cook for a further 2 minutes.

Step 3 Stir in the mushrooms, galangal and chilli. Stir-fry for 2 minutes.

2. Stir in the baby corn and cook for 5 minutes, add the mange tout peas and continue cooking for 2 minutes.

3. Stir in the mushrooms, galangal and chilli and stir-fry for 2 minutes. Sprinkle with the fish and soy sauce and serve.

Cook's Notes

Time
Preparation takes 10 minutes and cooking takes about 10 minutes.

Cook's Tip
This could be served as a vegetarian main course for 2 if the sauce is omitted.

LONG BEANS IN COCONUT MILK

In this recipe long beans are lightly cooked so
that they are still slightly crunchy when served.
SERVES 4-6

460g/1lb long beans
1 tbsp oil
2 stems lemon grass, sliced
2.5cm/1-inch piece galangal, sliced into thin sticks
1 large red chilli, seeded and chopped
280ml/½ pint thin coconut milk
Chilli 'flowers', to garnish

Step 1 Cut the beans
into 5cm/2-inch
pieces.

1. Top and tail the beans and cut into 5cm/2-inch pieces.

2. Heat the oil in a wok and stir-fry the lemon grass,
galangal and chilli for 1 minute.

3. Add the coconut milk and bring to the boil. Boil

for 3 minutes.

4. Stir in the beans, reduce the heat and simmer for
6 minutes. Garnish with chilli 'flowers' and serve
immediately.

Step 2 Stir-fry the
lemon grass,
galangal and chilli for
1 minute.

Step 3 Add the
coconut milk to the
wok. Bring to the boil
and boil for 3
minutes.

Cook's Notes

Time
Preparation takes 10 minutes
and cooking takes 7 minutes.

Variation
Substitute mange tout peas for
the beans and reduce the cooking
time to 2-3 minutes.

SAUTÉED BEAN SPROUTS

A simple vegetable dish which can be served with a
hot dipping sauce if wished or as a foil to a hot curry.

SERVES 4

2 tbsps oil
8 spring onions, thickly sliced
340g/12oz bean sprouts, rinsed and drained
120g/4oz cooked, peeled prawns, (optional)
½ small head of Chinese cabbage, shredded
1 tbsp fish sauce

1. Heat the oil in a wok until sizzling then add the spring onions, bean sprouts and prawns, if using. Stir-fry for 1-2 minutes.

2. Add the Chinese cabbage and toss over a high heat

Step 2 Add the Chinese cabbage and toss over a high heat for about 1 minute or until just beginning to wilt.

for about 1 minute or until just beginning to wilt.

3. Stir in the fish sauce and serve immediately with a dipping sauce of your choice.

Step 1 Stir-fry the spring onions, bean sprouts and prawns in the sizzling oil for 1-2 minutes.

Step 3 Stir in the fish sauce and serve immediately.

Cook's Notes

Time
Preparation takes 5 minutes and cooking takes 5 minutes.

Cook's Tip
Use fresh bean sprouts rather than canned for this recipe.

CUCUMBER SALAD

Salads are an important part of a Thai meal. They are usually carefully arranged rather than simply tossed together.

SERVES 4

1 cucumber
Few salad leaves, washed
1 red pepper, sliced
30g/1oz roasted peanuts

Dressing
2 tbsps lime juice
1 tbsp fish sauce
1 tsp sugar
1 small red or green chilli, seeded and chopped
2 tsps chopped coriander leaves

1. Cut the cucumber in half lengthways and scoop out the seeds with a teaspoon.

2. Cut the cucumber into slices about 5mm/¼-inch thick.

3. Arrange the lettuce leaves on a serving plate and then scatter the sliced pepper around the edge. Pile the cucumber into the centre. Sprinkle with the roasted peanuts.

4. To make the dressing, whisk all the ingredients together with a fork or place in a small screw-top jar and shake well.

5. Just before serving drizzle the dressing over the salad.

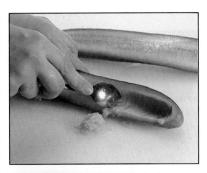

Step 1 Cut the cucumber in half lengthways and scoop out the seeds with a teaspoon.

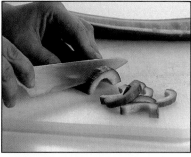

Step 2 Cut the cucumber crosswise into slices about 5mm/¼-inch thick.

Step 4 To make the dressing, whisk all the ingredients together with a fork or place in a small screw-top jar and shake well.

Cook's Notes

Time
Preparation takes 10 minutes.

Cook's Tip
Do not add the dressing to the salad until serving time.

GREEN PAPAYA SALAD

Originating in the north east of Thailand this dish is now popular countrywide.

SERVES 4-6

1 tbsp dried shrimps
4 small green chillies, sliced
3 cloves garlic, crushed
1 shallot, chopped
1 hard green papaya
1 tsp palm sugar
2 tbsps fish sauce
2 tbsps tamarind juice

Step 3 Cut the papaya in half, remove the seeds and peel with a vegetable peeler.

Step 1 Grind the dried shrimps in a pestle and mortar until well crushed.

Step 3 Grate the papaya flesh into a mixing bowl.

1. Place the dried shrimps in a pestle and mortar and grind until well crushed, remove and set aside.

2. Place the chillies, garlic and shallot in the pestle and mortar and pound until the ingredients are well bruised and their juices begin to blend.

3. Cut the papaya in half and remove the seeds. Peel, using a vegetable peeler, and grate the papaya flesh into a mixing bowl.

4. Combine the sugar, fish sauce and tamarind juice and stir until the sugar dissolves.

5. Add to the papaya along with the chilli mixture and toss together until well combined. Chill until required.

6. Transfer to a serving dish and sprinkle with the crushed shrimps just before serving.

Cook's Notes

Time
Preparation takes 20 minutes plus chilling.

Preparation
Use a coarse grater for preparing the papaya.

MIXED VEGETABLE STIR-FRY

Very fresh vegetables cooked quickly and
simply play a large part in Thai cuisine.

SERVES 4

Prik Dong
6 red or green chillies
90ml/6 tbsps white wine vinegar

2 tbsps oil
3 cloves garlic, crushed
1 shallot, sliced
90g/3oz each cauliflower and broccoli divided into
   small florets
1 small red pepper, sliced
120g/4oz mange tout peas
120g/4oz baby corn
120g/4oz long beans, cut into 5cm/2-inch lengths
2 carrots, peeled and sliced
90g/3oz straw mushrooms
2 tsps palm sugar
1 tbsp light soy sauce

Step 1 Slice the
chillies diagonally.

Step 2 Heat the oil in
a large wok and add
all the vegetables at
once. Stir-fry for 4
minutes.

Step 4 Add the sugar
and soy to the wok,
toss well and serve.

1. Slice the chillies diagonally and combine with the
vinegar in a small bowl. Use as a dipping sauce for the
vegetables.

2. Heat the oil in a wok and add all the vegetables at
once.

3. Stir-fry for 4 minutes until the vegetables are cooked
but still crisp.

4. Stir the sugar into the soy sauce and add to the wok,
toss well and serve. Serve with the dipping sauce.

Cook's Notes

Time
Preparation takes 15 minutes
and cooking takes 4-6 minutes.

Cook's Tip
Use the dipping sauce with
noodles as well as vegetables.

TOFU SALAD

This dish can also be served hot – return the tofu to the wok
and heat through, then serve immediately.

SERVES 4

90ml/6 tbsps oil
225g/8oz tofu, cubed
2 cloves garlic, crushed
120g/4oz broccoli florets
120g/4oz mange tout peas
1 tbsp soy sauce
1 tsp salted black beans
½ tsp palm sugar
90ml/6 tbsps vegetable stock
½ tsp cornflour

1. Heat the oil in a wok and fry the tofu until golden on all sides. Remove with a slotted spoon and cool, then refrigerate until required.

2. Pour off most of the oil. Add the garlic and fry until softened. Stir in the broccoli and mange tout, and stir-fry until just tender.

Step 2 Stir-fry the broccoli and mange tout until just tender.

Step 3 Add the soy, black beans and sugar and fry for 1 minute.

3. Add the soy, black beans and sugar and fry for 1 minute.

4. Mix a little of the stock with the cornflour and add the remaining stock and cornflour mixture to the wok. Cook until the sauce thickens slightly.

5. Transfer to a serving dish and chill until required. To serve, scatter the tofu cubes over the cooked vegetables.

Step 4 Blend a little of the stock with the cornflour and add to the wok with the rest of the stock. Cook until the sauce thickens slightly.

Cook's Notes

Time
Preparation takes 15 minutes and cooking takes about 10 minutes.

Variation
Use smoked tofu for a stronger flavour. Cooked chicken could be substituted for the tofu for a 'meat' version.

Chapter 6
Desserts

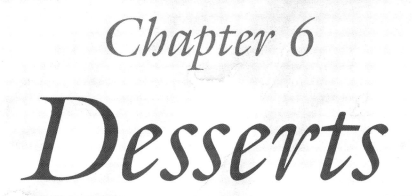

THAI FRUIT PLATTER WITH COCONUT SAUCE

Usually a Thai meal will finish with fresh fruit. In this recipe a selection of fruit is served with a simple coconut sauce.

SERVES 4

Selection of Thai fruit such as:
Lychees
Rambutans
Mango
Pineapple
Watermelon
Honey dew melon
Papaya
Star fruit
Bananas

Coconut Sauce
175ml/6 fl oz thick coconut milk
60g/2oz caster sugar

1. Prepare the fruit. Peel lychees or rambutans, starting at the stem end.

2. Cut mango in half either side of the stone, peel and slice into fingers.

3. Cut the pineapple into wedges, peeled if wished.

4. Cut melons and papaya in half and discard the seeds. Peel and slice.

5. Slice star fruit crosswise.

6. Cut bananas diagonally into chunks and toss in some lemon juice.

7. Arrange the fruit on a serving platter.

8. Make the sauce by combining the coconut milk and sugar. Pour over the fruit or serve separately in a bowl or jug.

Step 1 Peel lychees, starting at the stem end.

Step 2 Cut mango in half either side of the stone. Peel the fruit and slice the flesh into fingers.

Step 4 Cut the papaya in half and discard the seeds. Peel and slice the flesh.

Cook's Notes

Time
Preparation takes 20-30 minutes.

Cook's Tip
Chill the fruit and coconut sauce before serving if wished.

STICKY RICE WITH MANGO AND STAR FRUIT

Sweet, glutinous rice is served in many forms as a dessert in Thailand.
This delicious version is served with mango and star fruit.

SERVES 4

225g/8oz glutinous rice
420ml/¾ pint thick coconut milk
90g/3oz sugar
Pinch of salt
1 mango
1 star fruit

Step 1 Soak the rice overnight in cold water.

1. Soak the rice overnight in cold water.

2. Line the top of a steamer with muslin. Drain the rice and place in the steamer. Cover and steam for 25 minutes. The rice should be just tender but not fully cooked.

3. Combine the coconut milk, sugar and salt in a saucepan and heat gently. Stir in the steamed rice and simmer for 2 minutes.

Step 2 Line the top of a steamer with muslin. Add the drained rice, cover and steam for 25 minutes.

4. Remove from the heat, cover and leave to stand for 15 minutes. The rice will continue to cook in this time.

5. Cut the mango in half as close to the stone as possible. Remove the peel, and slice the flesh. Slice the star fruit crosswise.

6. Arrange the fruit and rice attractively on serving dishes.

Step 3 Add the steamed rice to the hot coconut milk, sugar and salt in the saucepan. Cover and simmer for 2 minutes then remove from the heat and leave to stand for 15 minutes.

Cook's Notes

Time
Preparation takes 10 minutes, plus overnight soaking. Cooking takes 27 minutes, plus 15 minutes standing.

Cook's Tip
Serve this dish with any other exotic fruit that you like.

THAI COCONUT CUSTARDS

This is one of the best known and most loved Thai desserts.

SERVES 6

4 eggs
420ml/¾ pint thick coconut milk
120g/4oz caster sugar
½ tsp jasmine water
Desiccated coconut, lime zest and twists, to decorate

1. Place the eggs, coconut milk, sugar and jasmine water in a bowl and whisk together until slightly frothy.

2. Pour into a shallow heat-proof dish that will fit into the top of a steamer.

3. Steam over gently simmering water for 30-40 minutes or until the custard is just set. If the custard cooks too quickly it will become rubbery in texture.

4. Remove from the steamer and allow to cool. Cut into wedges or blocks and decorate with the coconut, grated lime zest and lime twists.

Step 1 Place the eggs, coconut milk, sugar and jasmine water in a bowl and whisk together until slightly frothy.

Step 2 Pour the mixture into a shallow heat-proof dish that will fit into the top of a steamer.

Step 3 Steam the custard over gently simmering water for 30-40 minutes or until just set.

Cook's Notes

🕐 **Time**
Preparation takes 5 minutes and cooking takes 30-40 minutes.

◩ **Preparation**
The custard is cooked when the tip of a knife blade inserted into the centre comes out clean.

BLACK STICKY RICE

Look out for this rice in Thai or Oriental food stores.
If unavailable, substitute white sticky rice.

SERVES 6

175g/6oz black glutinous rice
1.1 litres/2 pints water
150g/5oz granulated sugar
420ml/¾ pint thick coconut milk
90g/3oz grated fresh coconut flesh

1. Rinse the rice under plenty of running water and drain well.

2. Place the rice in a large saucepan with the measured water. Bring gently to the boil, stir and reduce the heat. Simmer for 45 minutes or until rice is tender, stirring occasionally.

3. If the rice is tender and any water is left, drain off and discard. If the rice is not tender but there is not enough water, add a little more and continue until the rice is

Step 4 Stir in 90g/3oz of the sugar and 280ml/½ pint of the coconut milk and simmer gently for 10 minutes.

cooked. Transfer to a clean pan.

4. Stir in 90g/3oz of the sugar and 280ml/½ pint of the coconut milk; simmer gently for 10 minutes.

5. Combine the remaining sugar and coconut milk with the coconut flesh in a small pan and heat gently.

6. Spoon the rice into serving bowls and top with the coconut mixture. Serve at once.

Step 3 When the rice is cooked and tender, drain if necessary and transfer to a clean pan.

Step 5 Combine the remaining sugar, coconut milk and coconut flesh in a small pan and heat gently.

Cook's Notes

Time
Preparation takes 15 minutes and cooking takes 55 minutes.

Variation
To make chocolate sticky rice, add cocoa powder to taste with the coconut milk and sugar in Step 4.

COCONUT AND BANANA PANCAKES

These pancakes are delicious served warm or cold.

SERVES 4

120g/4oz rice flour
Pinch salt
2 eggs
280ml/½ pint thin coconut milk
Green food colouring (optional)
30g/1oz shredded or desiccated coconut

Filling
2 tbsps lime juice
Grated rind of ½ lime
1 tsp sugar
1 tbsp shredded or desiccated coconut
2 bananas

Oil for frying

1. Place the flour and the salt in a mixing bowl and make a well in the centre. Drop in the eggs and a little of the coconut milk.

2. Using a wooden spoon beat well, slowly incorporating the flour until you have a smooth, thick paste.

3. Gradually beat in the remaining coconut milk. Stir in a few drops of food colouring. Allow to stand for 20 minutes.

4. Meanwhile, make the filling. Mix together the lime juice, rind, sugar and coconut. Slice the bananas and toss in the mixture.

5. Stir the coconut into the pancake batter and heat a little oil in a 20.5cm/8 inch heavy-based frying pan. Pour off the excess and spoon in about 60ml/4 tbsps of the batter. Swirl to coat the pan. Cook for about 1 minute or until the underside is golden.

Step 1 Place the flour and salt in a mixing bowl and make a well in the centre. Drop in the eggs and a little of the milk.

Step 3 Gradually beat in the remaining coconut milk.

Step 5 Spoon about 60ml/4 tbsps of pancake batter into the pan and swirl to coat.

6. Flip or toss the pancake over and cook other side. Slide the pancake out of the pan and keep warm. Repeat until all the batter is used. Fill the pancakes with the banana mixture and serve immediately.

Cook's Notes

Time
Preparation takes 15 minutes, plus 20 minutes standing time. Cooking takes 15 minutes.

Serving Idea
Fold the pancakes into quarters and spoon some filling inside or divide filling between the pancakes and roll up.

MANGO ICE CREAM

The cool, smooth, creaminess of this delicious ice cream
makes it the perfect end to a Thai meal.

SERVES 8

420ml/¾ pint thick coconut milk
3 egg yolks
60ml/4 tbsps sugar
280ml/½ pint double cream
3 mangoes, peeled and stoned
Toasted flaked almonds, to decorate

1. Heat the coconut milk in a saucepan until very hot, but not boiling.

2. Beat together the egg yolks and sugar in a bowl, add

Step 2 Beat together the egg yolks and sugar in a bowl. Add a few spoons of the hot coconut milk and stir well.

Step 3 Cook the custard over a saucepan of simmering water, stirring constantly, until it coats the back of a spoon.

a few spoons of the hot coconut milk and stir well.

3. Stir into the remaining coconut milk and cook gently over a saucepan of simmering water, stirring constantly until it thickens enough to coat the back of a spoon.

4. Remove from the heat and cool. Whip the double cream until soft peaks form, then stir in the cooled custard.

5. Chop a little of the mango into small pieces and purée the remainder in a food processor or push through a sieve.

6. Fold the mango purée and chopped mango into the custard. Pour into a shallow, freezer-proof dish and freeze until slushy.

7. Remove from the freezer and process in the food processor or beat with an electric whisk until smooth. Freeze and beat once more then transfer to a freezer container and cover with a lid. Freeze until solid.

8. Remove the ice cream about 20-30 minutes before serving and allow to soften in the refrigerator. Scoop into dishes and serve sprinkled with toasted flaked almonds.

Step 6 Fold the mango purée and chopped mango into the custard.

Cook's Notes

Time
Preparation takes 30 minutes and cooking takes 10 minutes. Freezing takes several hours.

Preparation
Do not allow the coconut milk to boil as the eggs will curdle when added.

Cook's Tip
Beating the ice cream as it freezes breaks up the ice crystals and makes the texture of the ice cream smoother.

BANANAS IN COCONUT MILK

If you use the small, hard Thai bananas increase the
cooking time so that the banana is cooked until just tender.

SERVES 6

570ml/1 pint thin coconut milk
120g/4oz caster sugar
Pinch salt
6 small bananas
Toasted desiccated coconut, to decorate

1. Combine the coconut milk, caster sugar and salt in a wok or saucepan and heat gently, stirring until the sugar dissolves. Bring to the boil and boil rapidly for 5 minutes.

2. Cut the bananas in half or into chunks and place in the coconut milk. Reduce the heat and simmer gently

Step 1 Combine the milk, caster sugar and salt in a wok and heat gently, stirring until the sugar dissolves.

Step 1 Bring the mixture to the boil and boil rapidly for 5 minutes.

for 2-3 minutes or until the bananas are just soft.

3. Allow the mixture to cool and serve slightly warm or cold, sprinkled with the coconut.

Step 2 Add the banana chunks to the coconut milk and simmer for 2-3 minutes or until the bananas are just soft.

Cook's Notes

Time
Preparation takes 10 minutes and cooking takes 12 minutes.

Buying Guide
Buy slightly green bananas for this dish.

TAPIOCA WITH GOLDEN THREADS

Golden threads are used to decorate desserts, as in this case, or
enjoyed on their own with coffee.

SERVES 6

Golden Threads
6 egg yolks
280ml/½ pint water
275g/10oz granulated sugar

Tapioca
570ml/1 pint thin coconut milk
90g/3oz pearl tapioca, rinsed
30g/1oz palm sugar

1. To make the golden threads, puncture the base of a paper or plastic cup 3 or 4 times with a knitting needle or skewer.

2. Stir the egg yolks together and leave in the refrigerator until required.

3. Place the water and sugar in a wok or saucepan and heat stirring until the sugar dissolves. Bring to the boil, then reduce the heat to maintain a gentle boil.

4. Pour about one-third to a half of the egg yolk mixture into the cup whilst holding it over the saucepan of sugar and water. Let the yolks flow through the holes in the cup, in a steady stream. Move the cup slowly, from side to side so that the yolk forms strings.

5. As the yolk mixture hits the water it will cook. When set remove it with a skewer, fold into bundles and place on a plate. Repeat with the remaining egg, and chill until required.

6. To make the tapioca, place the coconut milk and tapioca in a saucepan, stir in the sugar and cook over a low heat for 30 minutes, stirring occasionally until the

Step 1 Puncture the base of a paper or plastic cup 3 or 4 times.

Step 4 Pour one-third of the egg yolk mixture into the cup whilst holding it over the saucepan of sugar and water. Let yolks flow through the holes in a steady stream. Move cup slowly from side to side so that the yolk forms strings.

Step 5 When the ribbons of egg yolk are set remove with a skewer and fold into bundles.

tapioca is tender. Spoon into dishes and arrange the golden threads on top.

Cook's Notes

Time
Preparation takes 20 minutes and cooking takes 45 minutes.

Serving Idea
Serve any spare golden threads with coffee.

Index